Cycle

CW00740381

Tours

Around Oxford: the Cotswolds, the Chilterns & the Ridgeway

Nick Cotton

Publisher: Cycle Tours is a joint venture between CycleCity Guides and Cordee

CycleCity Guides
The Welsh Mill
Parkhill Drive
Frome
BA11 2LE
T: +44 (0)1373 453533

info@cyclecityguides.co.uk
www.cyclecityguides.co.uk

Cordee
11 Jacknell Road
Dodwells Bridge Industrial Estate
Hinckley
LE10 3BS
T: +44 (0)1455 611 185

charlie@cordee.co.uk
www.cordee.co.uk

ISBN: 978-1904207573

Printed by: Victoria Litho
Picture credits: Nick Cotton

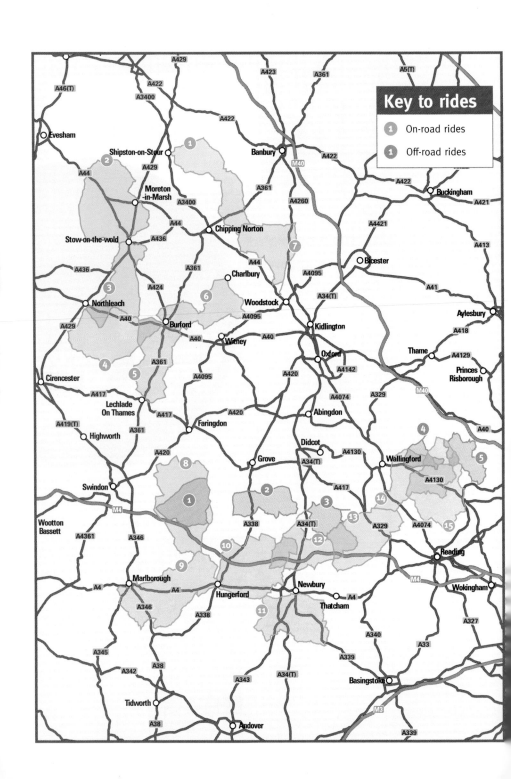

Quick reference chart

On-road rides

Ride number & title	Page	Distance	Grade
1 Shipston & the Tews	8	33m (53km)	▲▲▲
2 Moreton & Stow-on-the-Wold	14	30m (48km)	▲▲▲▲
3 Northleach & Stow-on-the-Wold	20	30m (48km)	▲▲▲
4 Burford & Northleach	26	29m (47km)	▲▲
5 Burford & Lechlade	32	29m (47km)	▲
6 Burford & Charlbury	38	30m (48km)	▲▲
7 Woodstock & the Tews	44	28m (45km)	▲▲
8 Lambourn & the Downs	50	30m (48km)	▲▲▲
9 Hungerford & Marlborough	56	37m (59km)	▲▲▲
10 Hungerford & the Downs	62	31m (50km)	▲▲
11 Kingsclere & Newbury	68	29m (47km)	▲▲▲
12 East Ilsley, Boxford & Frilsham	74	34m (54km)	▲▲▲
13 Goring & Pangbourne	80	26m (42km)	▲▲▲
14 Goring & Chiltern woodlands	86	32m (52km)	▲▲▲▲
15 West of Henley	92	29m (47km)	▲▲▲▲

Off-road rides

Ride number & title	Page	Distance	Grade
1 Lambourn & Uffington Castle	98	18m (30km)	▲▲▲
2 West Ilsley & the Ridgeway	102	20m (32km)	▲▲▲▲
3 Streatley & East Ilsley	108	17m (28km)	▲▲▲
4 Watlington & Maidensgrove	112	15m (24km)	▲▲▲▲▲
5 Hambleden & the heart of the Chilterns	116	18m (30km)	▲▲▲▲▲

Grades

▲	Easy	
▲▲	Easy / Moderate	The grade is based on the amount of climbing
▲▲▲	Moderate	involved and, for off-road routes, the roughness
▲▲▲▲	Moderate / Strenuous	of the surface rather than the distance covered.
▲▲▲▲▲	Strenuous	

Around Oxford: the Cotswolds, the Chilterns & the Ridgeway

Cycling in the countryside around Oxford presents something of a conundrum: the city itself is one of the most cycle-friendly in the country with thousands of cyclists using their bikes every day to get to school, university or work. However, further afield, much of the area is dominated by busy roads and there are often gaps in the lane network meaning it is hard to cross A roads safely. Never fear! By casting the net a little wider and by exploring the area further west towards the Cotswolds, southeast towards the Chilterns and south to the Lambourn Downs and the Ridgeway, it is quite possible to devise routes that offer all that one would want from an enjoyable bike ride: quiet lanes, pretty villages, good pubs and cafés and the absolute minimum of time spent on roads heavy with traffic.

Seven of the road rides explore the honey-stone villages lying to the west and northwest of Oxford, from Woodstock through the beautiful Tew and Sibford villages as far as Chipping Campden and from Minster Lovell and Burford along the lovely Windrush and Coln valleys towards Northleach and Bibury. This is an area full of lovely old stone buildings dating back to the 17th and 18th centuries; the wealth to build them came from the medieval wool and cloth trade. The rides venture as far as the escarpment at Broadway Tower and visit the handsome towns of Stow-on-the-Wold, Moreton-in-Marsh and Bourton-on-the-Water as well as countless smaller villages, often with a pub and sometimes a tearoom as well.

To the south, five of the road rides link together quiet lanes across the chalk downlands between the Vale of the White Horse and the Kennet & Avon Canal. This is a land of small villages, big open arable fields and a high likelihood of seeing race horses training on the gallops over the Lambourn Downs.

The Chiltern beechwoods lie to the southeast of Oxford and three of the rides use the dense network of lanes that criss-cross the area around Goring, Pangbourne and Henley. Rides here take on an extraordinary beauty in late spring when the woodland floor is carpeted with bluebells and the beechwoods are coming into leaf, almost glowing with translucent green, and also through autumn with the changing of the colours.

Three of the off-road rides are located on or around the chalk and flint tracks of the Ridgeway, claimed to be the oldest road in Europe, dating back 5000 years. The other two rides delve deep into the beech woodlands of the Chilterns. As with so much off-road riding in Southern England, try to leave these for late spring to late autumn after a dry spell, as the trails can get very sticky in winter and after prolonged rain.

Other useful information

Easy, traffic-free cycling for families and novices

Although the rides in this book are aimed at reasonably fit cyclists who are happy riding on roads or, in the case of mountain bikers, happy to ride on rough tracks, there may be times when your preference is for a ride that is also suitable for children or 'novice' cyclists. Listed below are some of the easier, flatter, traffic-free routes in the area.

Canals & rivers

1. The River Thames through Oxford
There is a wide smooth cyclepath alongside the River Thames from Jericho / Port Meadow (northwest of Oxford city centre) that runs south to the Ring Road (A423) to link with a traffic-free path as far as the Kennington - Radley road. This forms part of National Cycle Network Route 5 from Oxford to Reading, which is a mixture of traffic-free sections and quiet lanes. See: **www.oxfordshire.gov.uk** and search **'Cycling Maps'**. For the route from Oxford to Didcot go to **www.sustrans.org** and search **'Hanson Way'** or go to their online mapping.

2. Reading to Sonning
You can ride traffic-free alongside the Kennet & Avon Canal to the west of Reading and alongside the River Thames east from Reading to Sonning: **www.reading.gov.uk/cycling**

3. Kennet & Avon Canal
Many stretches of the canal towpath (which runs from Bath to Reading) are suitable for recreational cycling. A long section is used through Newbury on Ride 11. See: **www.sustrans.org.uk** or **www.waterscape.com** and search **'Kennet & Avon Canal'**.

Railway paths

1. Phoenix Trail
7-mile trail between Thame and Princes Risborough. See: **www.sustrans.org.uk** or **www.chilternsaonb.org** and search **'Phoenix Trail'**.

2. Marlborough & Chiseldon
7-mile trail between Marlborough and Chiseldon. The northern part of the trail is shown on: **www.forestweb.org.uk/gwf-leisure.pdf**

Woodland

1. Look Out, Bracknell
A 2600-acre Crown Estate woodland with waymarked trails. See: **www.bracknell-forest.gov.uk/lookout** and click on **'Outdoor activities'**.

2. Wendover Woods
Steep woodland with waymarked 'family' trails and a good café at the top. See: **www.forestry.gov.uk/WendoverWoods**

Other

1. Windsor Great Park
Several almost traffic-free roads within the Great Park. See: **www.thecrownestate.co.uk/windsor_great_park**

2. Milton Keynes
There is an extraordinary network of traffic-free trails along canals, through parkland and alongside the River Ouse. See: **www.mkweb.co.uk/cycling** or **www.destinationmiltonkeynes.co.uk/family_cycling**

3. Cotswold Water Park, south of Cirencester
Many tracks and trails between the man-made lakes in the water park. See: **www.waterpark.org/general/water_park_map.html**

Sustrans and the National Cycle Network

Go to **www.sustrans.org.uk** click on **'Sustrans near you'** then **'South East'** for Oxfordshire and Berkshire. There are downloads, details of free leaflets and details of NCN routes in the region.

Cycle shops in the area

See:
www.ioxfordshire.co.uk/local/cycle-shops/
www.iberkshire.co.uk/local/cycle-shops/
www.igloucestershire.co.uk/local/cycle-shops/
www.thecyclepeople.com

3

Legend to 1:50,000 maps

Roads & paths

Motorway

Service area (S) — M 1 — Elevated
Junction number [1]

Primary route

Unfenced — Dual carriageway
A 470

Main road

Footbridge
A 493

Road under construction

Secondary road

B 4518

Narrow road with passing places

A 855 — B 885

Road generally more than 4m wide

Bridge

Road generally less than 4m wide

Other road

Path

Gradient: 1 in 5 and steeper. 1 in 7 to 1 in 5

Gates — Road tunnel

Passenger ferry — Vehicle ferry
Ferry P — Ferry V

Tourist information

⚔ 🚐 / ⚔🏕	Camp site / caravan site
❋	Garden
⚑	Golf course or links
i i	Information centre, all year / seasonal
🦆	Nature reserve
P P&R / P&R	Parking / Park & Ride, all year / seasonal
✕	Picnic site
▨	Selected place of tourist interest
☎	Public telephone
☎	Roadside assistance
🔆	Viewpoint
V	Visitor centre
❗	Walks / Trails
▲	Youth hostel
⊘	World Heritage site / area
⊗	Recreation / leisure / sports centre

Railways

——————	Track multiple or single
— — —	Track under construction
+++++++	Light rapid transit system, narrow gauge or tramway
⫻⊬⊬⫻	Bridge, footbridge
⊐⊐⊐···⊏⊏⊏	Tunnel, cutting
●■ᵃ	Station, (a) principal
——————	Siding
+—○—+	Light rapid transit system station
‖ LC	Level crossing
⫿⫿⟋⟍⫿⫿	Viaduct, embankment

Water features

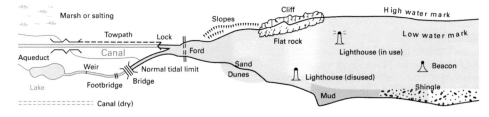

Marsh or salting · Slopes · Cliff · High water mark
Towpath · Lock · Flat rock · Low water mark
Aqueduct · Canal · Ford · Lighthouse (in use)
Weir · Normal tidal limit · Sand · Beacon
Lake · Footbridge · Bridge · Dunes · Lighthouse (disused) · Shingle
Canal (dry) · Mud

4

General features

⫯⫯⫯⫯⫯ ⫯⫯⫯⫯⫯	Cutting, embankment
	Landfill site
	Coniferous wood
	Non-coniferous wood
	Mixed wood
	Orchard
	Park or ornamental ground
	Forestry Commission land
	National Trust - always open
	National Trust - limited access, observe local signs
	National Trust for Scotland - always open
	National Trust for Scotland - limited access, observe local signs
⅄‒‒‒⅄‒‒‒⅄	Electricity transmission line (pylons shown at standard spacing)
> - -> - ->	Pipe line (arrow indicates direction of flow)
	Building
	Important building (selected)
	Bus or coach station
	Glass structure
Ⓗ	Hospital
	Place of worship with tower
	Place of worship with spire, dome or minaret
+	Place of worship
	Mast
	Wind pump / wind turbine
	Windmill with or without sails
+	Graticule intersection at 5' intervals

Rock features

Outcrop
650
Cliff
600
Scree

Public rights of way
(not applicable in Scotland)

⋯⋯⋯⋯	Footpath
⋅—⋅—⋅—⋅—	Restricted byway
— — — —	Bridleway
-+-+-+-+-	Byway open to all traffic

Public rights of way shown have been taken from local authority definitive maps and later amendments. The symbols show the defined route so far as the scale of mapping will allow.

The representation on this map of any other road, track or path is no evidence of the existence of a right of way.

Other public access

⋅ ⋅ ⋅ ⋅	Other route with public access
◆ ◆ ◆	National Trail, European Long Distance Path, Long Distance Route, selected Recreational Routes
● ● ●	On-road cycle route
○ ○ ○	Off-road cycle route
4	National Cycle Network Number
8	Regional Cycle Network Number
Danger Area	Firing and test ranges in the area Danger! Observe warning notices

Boundaries

+—+—+—+	National
⋅+⋅+⋅+⋅+	District
—⋅—⋅—⋅—	County, region or island area
	National Park

Abbreviations

CH	Clubhouse
PH	Public house
PC	Public convenience (in rural area)
TH	Town Hall, Guildhall or equivalent
CG	Cattle grid
P	Post office
MP	Milepost
MS	Mile stone

Antiquities

+	Position of antiquity that cannot be drawn to scale
☆ ⋯⋅	Visible earthwork
VILLA	Roman
Castle	Non-Roman
✕	Battlefield (with date)

Heights

—50—	Contours are at 10 metre vertical intervals
·144	Heights are to the nearest metre above mean sea level
	Heights shown close to a triangulation pillar refer to the station height at ground level and not necessarily to the summit

5

Abbreviations and instructions

Instructions are given concisely to make them easy to follow while out riding. Remember to read one or two instructions ahead so that you do not miss a turning. This is most likely when you have to turn off a road / track you have been following for a while and are marked **Easy to miss** to warn you.

If there appears to be a contradiction between the instructions and what you actually see, always refer to the map. There are many reasons why, over the course of time, instructions may be subject to change with new roads, new junctions and new signposts.

Directions (all directions are given in bold)

L	left
R	right
SA	straight ahead
bear **L** or **R**	a turn which is less than 90 degrees (right-angle) at a fork in the road or on a sharp bend so that your course appears to be straight ahead; this is often written as 'in effect **SA**'
sharp **L** or **R**	a turn more acute than a right-angle
L or **R** sharply back on yourself	almost a U-turn
R then **L**	normally a T-junction where the next turn is visible from the first
R then first **L**	the second turning may be some distance from the first, ie '**R** then after 1/2 mile first **L**'

Junctions

T-j	T-junction, a junction where you have to give way
X-roads	crossroads, a junction where you may or may not have to give way
offset X-roads	the four roads are not in the form of a perfect cross and you will have to turn left then right, or vice versa, to continue the route

Signs

'Placename 2'	the words in quotation marks are those that appear on the signs, the numbers indicate the distance in miles unless stated otherwise
(NS)	not signposted

Instructions

An example of an easy instruction is:

4 At T-j at end of Smith Road by the White Swan Inn turn **R** on Brown Street 'Greentown 2, Redville 3'

There is more information in this instruction than you would normally need but things do change: pubs may close down and signs may be replaced, removed or vandalised.

An example of a difficult instruction is:

8 **Easy to miss:** shortly after the brow of the hill, on fast descent, first **R** (NS)

As you can see, there is no T-junction or 'Give Way' sign to halt you in your tracks, no signpost indicating where the right turn will take you and in addition you are picking up speed on a downhill, so you need to have your wits about you not to miss the turning.

Overview pages

Start
This is the suggested start point, coinciding with Instruction 1 on the map. There is no reason why you should not start at another point if it is more convenient.

Busy roads
These rides aim to keep to an absolute minimum time spent on busy roads but there are sometimes unavoidable sections where lane networks do not neatly link together. These busy roads are mentioned so that you are mentally prepared to deal with traffic, especially if there are children or less experienced cyclists in the group.

Terrain
This brief description of the terrain covered by the route should be read in conjunction with the cross-profile diagram at the foot of the page to help you plan your journey.

Distance
The distance (shown in miles and kilometres) is, of course, that from the beginning to the end of the ride. However, if you wish to shorten the ride because of tiredness, mechanical problems, a change in the weather or simply lack of time then the maps enable you to do so.

Grade
There are five grades of difficulty:
Easy
Easy / Moderate
Moderate
Moderate / Strenuous
Strenuous
The grade is based on the amount of climbing involved and, for off-road routes, the roughness of the surface rather than the distance covered.

Map pages
Route overviews show how the maps have been laid out on the pages. Page numbers are shown in the corners. The diagrams show start points, route direction and some of the villages on or near the route.

Cross-profile
Shows heights in metres and distance travelled. Places along the route are shown.

Other rides nearby
Schematic map showing where nearby rides overlap. Shorter or longer rides can be created by mixing and matching rides.

Refreshments
More than three pubs or a mixture of pubs, cafés and tearooms in any one place is indicated by 'Lots of choice'. Otherwise, names of pubs, cafés and tearooms are listed, where possible with telephone numbers so that you can call ahead to check on opening times and when food is served.

Shipston-on-Stour, the Sibfords & the Tews

Lying to the east of the Cotswolds and to the west of the Cherwell valley is a rolling arable landscape filled with attractive yellow-stone villages such as the Sibfords, the Tews and Hook Norton. These are all linked together by using a fine network of quiet lanes thus almost entirely avoiding the busier roads which run between Oxford, Banbury, Stratford and Chipping Norton. A long and steady climb from Shipston, located in the Stour Valley, takes you to the highest point of the whole ride at The Warren to the west of Epwell. On your way up the hill you will catch glimpses of

Compton Wynyates, described by Pevsner as 'the most perfect picture-book house of Early Tudor decades'. It has been owned by the same family for over 800 years. It is not open to the public.

Drop down from the highpoint through the handsome villages of Sibford Gower and Sibford Ferris on your way to Great Tew, perhaps the prettiest of all the villages visited on the ride. Most of the cottages here, some of which have thatched roofs, date back to the 17th and 18th centuries and were built by Lord Falkland, after whom the village pub is named. There is also a café here. On your way back towards Shipston you pass through Hook Norton, home of the famous real ale. It is worth detouring a few hundred yards to see the brewery, housed in an extraordinary Victorian building made of bricks, cast iron, slate, timber and other materials.

Overview
On-road ● 33 miles / 53 kilometres ● Moderate

Start
Bridge Car Park, on the B4035 just east of Shipston (west of Banbury)

Parking
As above

Busy roads
A361 / B4022 between Wigginton and Great Tew
13 to **14**

Terrain
Undulating. The longest climb (525ft / 160m) is from the start to The Warren (west of Epwell), starting gently but with some steeper sections near the end

Nearest railway
Banbury, Moreton-in-Marsh or Charlbury

Other rides nearby

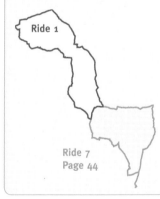

Ride 1

Ride 7
Page 44

Refreshments
Shipston-on-Stour
Lots of choice

Sibford Gower
Wykham Arms PH
T: 01295 788808

Wigginton
White Swan Inn
T: 01608 737322

Great Tew
Sweet Pea Coffee Shop
T: 01608 683693
Falkland Arms PH
T: 01608 683653
Baxters Coffee Shop
(south of village)
T: 01608 683896

Hook Norton
Lots of choice (four pubs)

Map pages

10 · 11
Shipston-on-Stour · Compton Wynyates · Willington · Sibford Gower · Traitor's Ford · Wigginton Heath · Hook Norton · Dunthrop · Great Tew
12 · 13

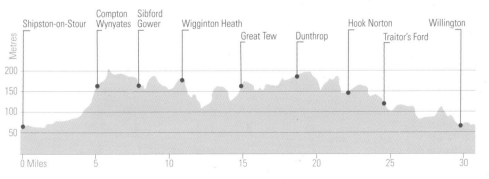

Shipston-on-Stour · Compton Wynyates · Sibford Gower · Wigginton Heath · Great Tew · Dunthrop · Hook Norton · Traitor's Ford · Willington

Metres
200
150
100
50

0 Miles · 5 · 10 · 15 · 20 · 25 · 30

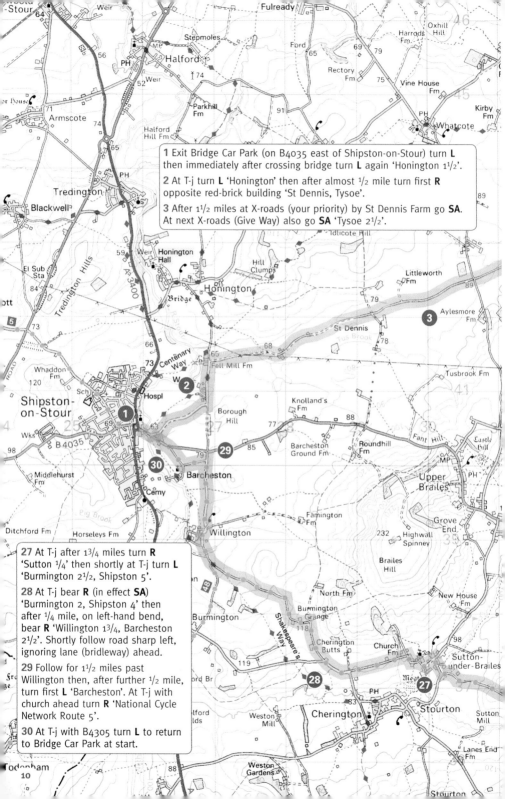

1 Exit Bridge Car Park (on B4035 east of Shipston-on-Stour) turn **L** then immediately after crossing bridge turn **L** again 'Honington 1½'.

2 At T-j turn **L** 'Honington' then after almost ½ mile turn first **R** opposite red-brick building 'St Dennis, Tysoe'.

3 After 1½ miles at X-roads (your priority) by St Dennis Farm go **SA**. At next X-roads (Give Way) also go **SA** 'Tysoe 2½'.

27 At T-j after 1¾ miles turn **R** 'Sutton ¼' then shortly at T-j turn **L** 'Burmington 2½, Shipston 5'.

28 At T-j bear **R** (in effect **SA**) 'Burmington 2, Shipston 4' then after ¼ mile, on left-hand bend, bear **R** 'Willington 1¾, Barcheston 2½'. Shortly follow road sharp left, ignoring lane (bridleway) ahead.

29 Follow for 1½ miles past Willington then, after further ½ mile, turn first **L** 'Barcheston'. At T-j with church ahead turn **R** 'National Cycle Network Route 5'.

30 At T-j with B4305 turn **L** to return to Bridge Car Park at start.

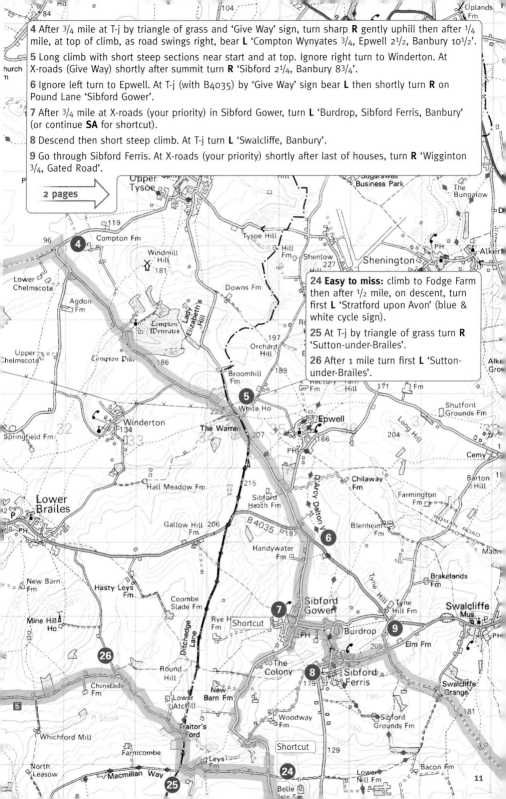

4 After 3/4 mile at T-j by triangle of grass and 'Give Way' sign, turn sharp **R** gently uphill then after 1/4 mile, at top of climb, as road swings right, bear **L** 'Compton Wynyates 3/4, Epwell 2 1/2, Banbury 10 1/2'.

5 Long climb with short steep sections near start and at top. Ignore right turn to Winderton. At X-roads (Give Way) shortly after summit turn **R** 'Sibford 2 1/4, Banbury 8 3/4'.

6 Ignore left turn to Epwell. At T-j (with B4035) by 'Give Way' sign bear **L** then shortly turn **R** on Pound Lane 'Sibford Gower'.

7 After 3/4 mile at X-roads (your priority) in Sibford Gower, turn **L** 'Burdrop, Sibford Ferris, Banbury' (or continue **SA** for shortcut).

8 Descend then short steep climb. At T-j turn **L** 'Swalcliffe, Banbury'.

9 Go through Sibford Ferris. At X-roads (your priority) shortly after last of houses, turn **R** 'Wigginton 3/4, Gated Road'.

2 pages ➡

24 Easy to miss: climb to Fodge Farm then after 1/2 mile, on descent, turn first **L** 'Stratford upon Avon' (blue & white cycle sign).

25 At T-j by triangle of grass turn **R** 'Sutton-under-Brailes'.

26 After 1 mile turn first **L** 'Sutton-under-Brailes'.

11

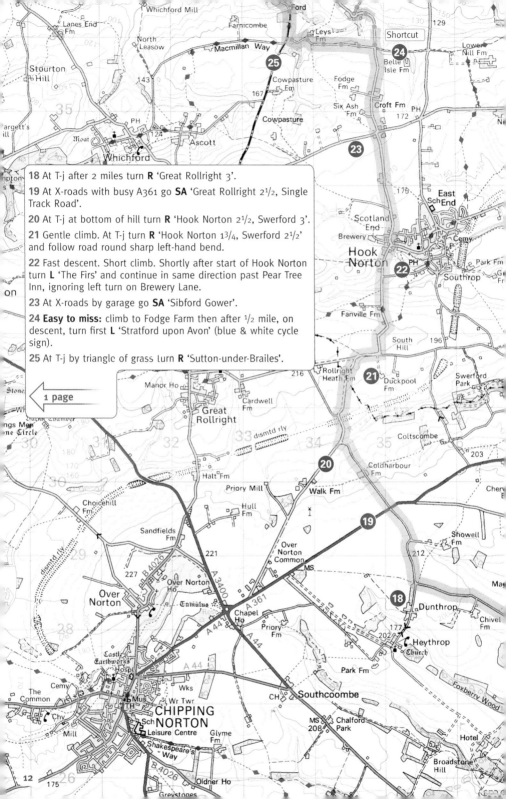

18 At T-j after 2 miles turn **R** 'Great Rollright 3'.

19 At X-roads with busy A361 go **SA** 'Great Rollright 2½, Single Track Road'.

20 At T-j at bottom of hill turn **R** 'Hook Norton 2½, Swerford 3'.

21 Gentle climb. At T-j turn **R** 'Hook Norton 1¾, Swerford 2½' and follow road round sharp left-hand bend.

22 Fast descent. Short climb. Shortly after start of Hook Norton turn **L** 'The Firs' and continue in same direction past Pear Tree Inn, ignoring left turn on Brewery Lane.

23 At X-roads by garage go **SA** 'Sibford Gower'.

24 Easy to miss: climb to Fodge Farm then after ½ mile, on descent, turn first **L** 'Stratford upon Avon' (blue & white cycle sign).

25 At T-j by triangle of grass turn **R** 'Sutton-under-Brailes'.

← 1 page

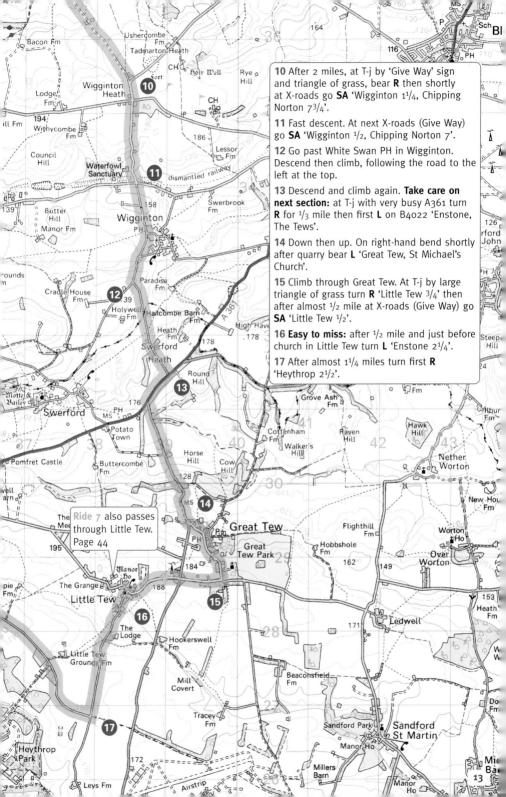

10 After 2 miles, at T-j by 'Give Way' sign and triangle of grass, bear **R** then shortly at X-roads go **SA** 'Wigginton 1¼, Chipping Norton 7¾'.

11 Fast descent. At next X-roads (Give Way) go **SA** 'Wigginton ½, Chipping Norton 7'.

12 Go past White Swan PH in Wigginton. Descend then climb, following the road to the left at the top.

13 Descend and climb again. **Take care on next section:** at T-j with very busy A361 turn **R** for ⅓ mile then first **L** on B4022 'Enstone, The Tews'.

14 Down then up. On right-hand bend shortly after quarry bear **L** 'Great Tew, St Michael's Church'.

15 Climb through Great Tew. At T-j by large triangle of grass turn **R** 'Little Tew ¾' then after almost ½ mile at X-roads (Give Way) go **SA** 'Little Tew ½'.

16 **Easy to miss:** after ½ mile and just before church in Little Tew turn **L** 'Enstone 2¼'.

17 After almost 1¼ miles turn first **R** 'Heythrop 2½'.

Ride 7 also passes through Little Tew. Page 44

13

The High Cotswolds from Moreton-in-Marsh to Chipping Campden & Stow-on-the-Wold

This ride starts from the attractive wide High Street of Moreton-in-Marsh, located near the source of the River Evenlode, one of the main tributaries of the Thames. It also lies on the course of the Fosse Way, one of the longest Roman roads in Britain, linking Exeter to Lincoln. Climb past the fine old buildings at Batsford where you may wish to visit the Arboretum and the Falconry Centre. You cross an important watershed: from the Evenlode which drains into the Thames and reaches the sea east of London, to the River Stour which joins the Avon then the Severn to reach the sea via the Bristol Channel. Chipping Campden is the next highlight. Its wealth was derived from the medieval wool trade. From here you are faced with one of the toughest climbs in the whole book, reaching a highpoint at over 1000ft at Broadway Tower, built in the late 1700s by the Earl of Coventry. On a clear day it is said that you can see 12 counties from the top of the tower. Descend through lovely broadleaf woodland, at one point passing a series of lavender fields. A second highpoint is on Cutsdean Hill as you continue south, close to the edge of the Cotswold escarpment. A long gentle descent past Cotswold Farm Park is followed by two climbs, the second on a short section of busier road, to bring you right into the heart of the handsome town of Stow-on-the-Wold, the highest hilltop town in the Cotswolds. Drop down to Broadwell and Evenlode and follow the River Evenlode northwards back to your starting point in Moreton-in-Marsh.

Overview
On-road ● 30 miles / 48 kilometres ● Moderate / Strenuous

Start
High Street, Moreton-in-Marsh

Parking
Plenty of street parking in the wide High Street

Busy roads
● There is a 30mph speed limit through Moreton-in-Marsh ❶

● The B4068 to the west of Stow ⓮ to ⓯

Terrain
Hilly with several climbs, the longest of which (570ft / 174m) lies between Chipping Campden and Broadway Tower

Nearest railway
Moreton-in-Marsh

Other rides nearby

Ride 2

Ride 3
Page 20

Refreshments
Moreton-in-Marsh
Lots of choice

Paxford
Churchill PH
T: 01386 594000

Chipping Campden
Lots of choice

Near Temple Guiting
Tearoom at Cotswold Farm Park
T: 01451 850307

Lower Swell
Golden Ball Inn
T: 01451 833886

Stow-on-the-Wold
Lots of choice

Broadwell
Fox Inn
T: 01451 870909

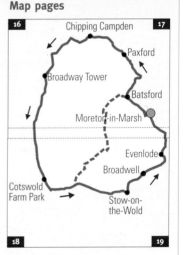

Map pages

16 Chipping Campden 17
Paxford
Broadway Tower
Batsford
Moreton-in-Marsh
Evenlode
Broadwell
Cotswold Farm Park
Stow-on-the-Wold
18 19

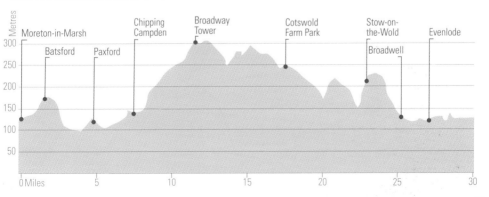

15

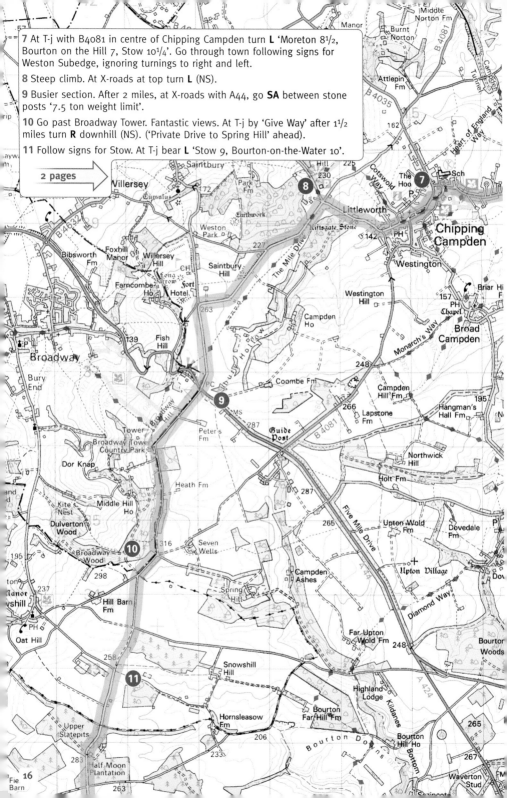

7 At T-j with B4081 in centre of Chipping Campden turn **L** 'Moreton 8½, Bourton on the Hill 7, Stow 10¼'. Go through town following signs for Weston Subedge, ignoring turnings to right and left.

8 Steep climb. At X-roads at top turn **L** (NS).

9 Busier section. After 2 miles, at X-roads with A44, go **SA** between stone posts '7.5 ton weight limit'.

10 Go past Broadway Tower. Fantastic views. At T-j by 'Give Way' after 1½ miles turn **R** downhill (NS). ('Private Drive to Spring Hill' ahead).

11 Follow signs for Stow. At T-j bear **L** 'Stow 9, Bourton-on-the-Water 10'.

2 pages

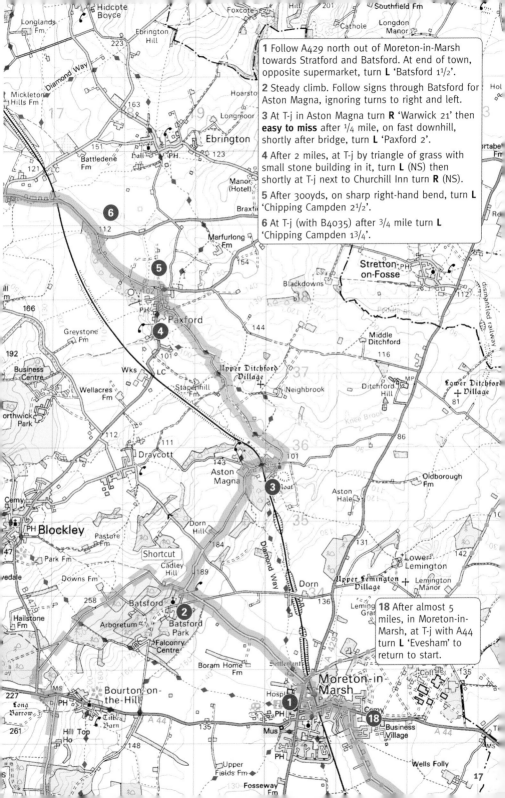

1 Follow A429 north out of Moreton-in-Marsh towards Stratford and Batsford. At end of town, opposite supermarket, turn **L** 'Batsford 1½'.

2 Steady climb. Follow signs through Batsford for Aston Magna, ignoring turns to right and left.

3 At T-j in Aston Magna turn **R** 'Warwick 21' then **easy to miss** after ¼ mile, on fast downhill, shortly after bridge, turn **L** 'Paxford 2'.

4 After 2 miles, at T-j by triangle of grass with small stone building in it, turn **L** (NS) then shortly at T-j next to Churchill Inn turn **R** (NS).

5 After 300yds, on sharp right-hand bend, turn **L** 'Chipping Campden 2½'.

6 At T-j (with B4035) after ¾ mile turn **L** 'Chipping Campden 1¾'.

18 After almost 5 miles, in Moreton-in-Marsh, at T-j with A44 turn **L** 'Evesham' to return to start.

12 After almost 3 miles, at X-roads with B4077, go **SA** 'The Slaughters 5, Bourton-on-the-Water 10'.

13 About ½ mile after Cotswold Farm Park turn **L** at X-roads (your priority) 'Stow, Lower Swell'.

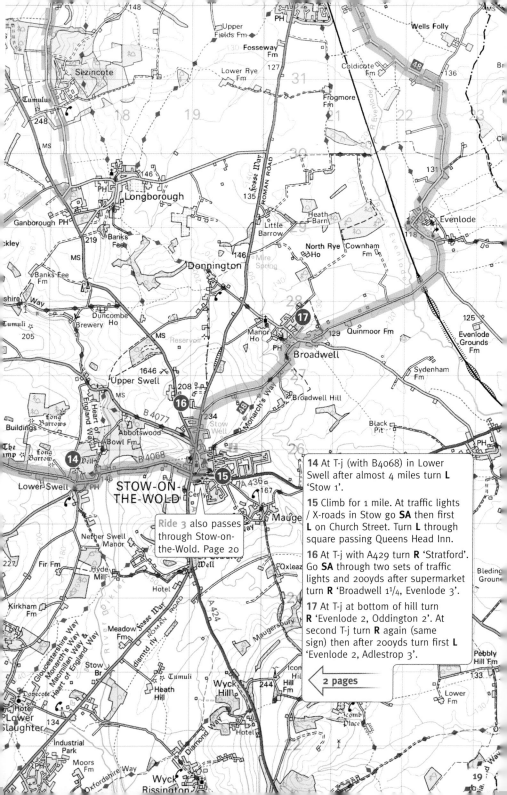

14 At T-j (with B4068) in Lower Swell after almost 4 miles turn **L** 'Stow 1'.

15 Climb for 1 mile. At traffic lights / X-roads in Stow go **SA** then first **L** on Church Street. Turn **L** through square passing Queens Head Inn.

16 At T-j with A429 turn **R** 'Stratford'. Go **SA** through two sets of traffic lights and 200yds after supermarket turn **R** 'Broadwell 1¼, Evenlode 3'.

17 At T-j at bottom of hill turn **R** 'Evenlode 2, Oddington 2'. At second T-j turn **R** again (same sign) then after 200yds turn first **L** 'Evenlode 2, Adlestrop 3'.

Ride 3 also passes through Stow-on-the-Wold. Page 20

2 pages

Northleach, Stow-on-the-Wold & the Windrush Valley

This ride links together Northleach, Bourton-on-the-Water and Stow-on-the-Wold, three of the most handsome towns in the Cotswolds, each with a large square or wide main street, surrounded by houses dating back to the 17th century. The fine church in Northleach was endowed by wool merchants in the 15th century; wool and the cloth trade generated fortunes through the Middle Ages and created the wealth that enabled the building of so many fine houses in the area. Bourton-on-the-Water is the most popular town in all the Cotswolds, thronged by coach parties and famous for its Model Village, built at ¹/₉th scale of the real village. You may prefer to pass gently through Bourton towards the quieter pastures of Lower Slaughter and Lower Swell. Bourton lies in the valley of the River Windrush and 'Wold' in Stow-on-the-Wold means 'hill', so it is no surprise to be faced with a tough climb taking you up to the stunning square in the middle of Stow. Descend eastwards through Maugersbury before regaining height at Wyck Beacon. A gentle descent over five miles

drops you back down into the Windrush Valley near to Great Barrington. This is followed west through Little Barrington and Windrush then along its tributary valley of Sherborne Brook to Farmington. A short steep final climb takes you under the A40 and back to Northleach.

Overview
On-road ● 30 miles / 48 kilometres ● Moderate

Start
Northleach, near the junction of the A40 and A429, about 10 miles east of Cheltenham

Parking
In Market Place / High Street

Busy roads
● B4068 west of Stow ⑩

● B4450 to the east of Stow ⑫ to ⑬

Terrain
Hilly with several climbs which follow the crossing of tributaries of the River Windrush. The longest climb (425ft / 130m), between Stow and Wyck Beacon, leads to a long ridge section

Nearest railway
Moreton-in-Marsh, about 4 miles north of Stow-on-the-Wold

Refreshments
Northleach
Lots of choice

Bourton-on-the-Water
Lots of choice

Lower Swell
Golden Ball Inn
T: 01451 833886

Stow-on-the-Wold
Lots of choice

Great Rissington
(just off the route)
Lamb Inn
T: 01451 820388

Great Barrington
Fox Inn
T: 01451 844385

Other rides nearby

Ride 2
Page 14

Ride 3

Ride 4
Page 26

Ride 5
Page 32

Map pages

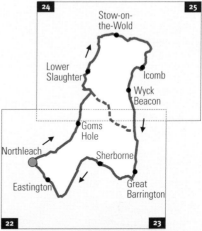

24   25
Stow-on-the-Wold
Lower Slaughter
Icomb
Wyck Beacon
Goms Hole
Northleach
Sherborne
Eastington
Great Barrington
22   23

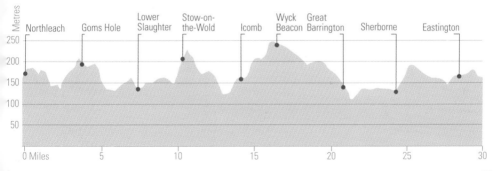

Metres

Northleach | Goms Hole | Lower Slaughter | Stow-on-the-Wold | Icomb | Wyck Beacon | Great Barrington | Sherborne | Eastington

250
200
150
100
50

0 Miles   5   10   15   20   25   30

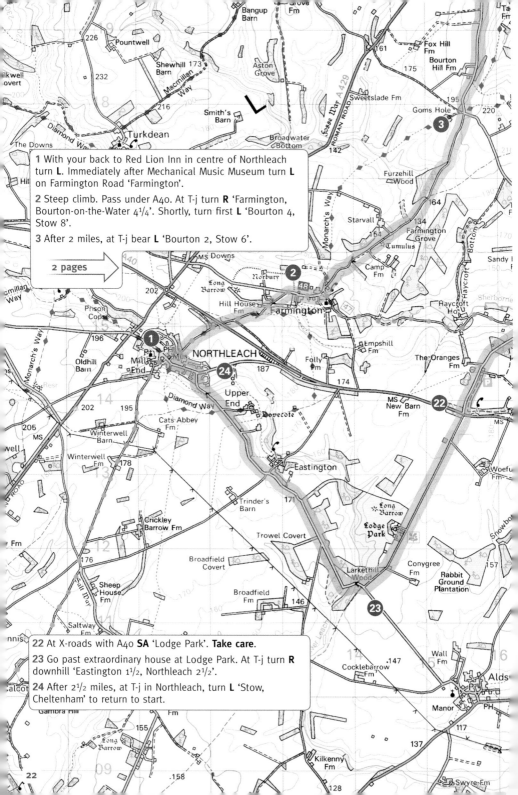

1 With your back to Red Lion Inn in centre of Northleach turn **L**. Immediately after Mechanical Music Museum turn **L** on Farmington Road 'Farmington'.

2 Steep climb. Pass under A40. At T-j turn **R** 'Farmington, Bourton-on-the-Water 4¼'. Shortly, turn first **L** 'Bourton 4, Stow 8'.

3 After 2 miles, at T-j bear **L** 'Bourton 2, Stow 6'.

2 pages ➡

22 At X-roads with A40 **SA** 'Lodge Park'. **Take care.**

23 Go past extraordinary house at Lodge Park. At T-j turn **R** downhill 'Eastington 1½, Northleach 2½'.

24 After 2½ miles, at T-j in Northleach, turn **L** 'Stow, Cheltenham' to return to start.

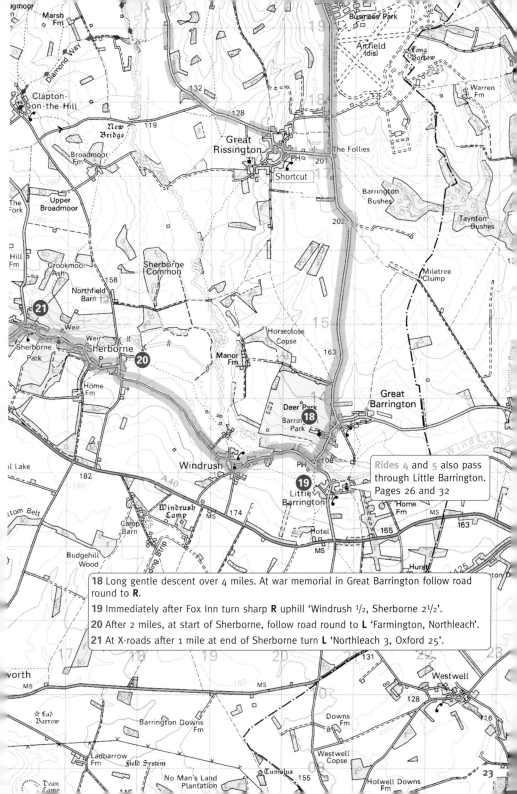

Rides 4 and 5 also pass
through Little Barrington.
Pages 26 and 32

18 Long gentle descent over 4 miles. At war memorial in Great Barrington follow road round to **R**.

19 Immediately after Fox Inn turn sharp **R** uphill 'Windrush ½, Sherborne 2½'.

20 After 2 miles, at start of Sherborne, follow road round to **L** 'Farmington, Northleach'.

21 At X-roads after 1 mile at end of Sherborne turn **L** 'Northleach 3, Oxford 25'.

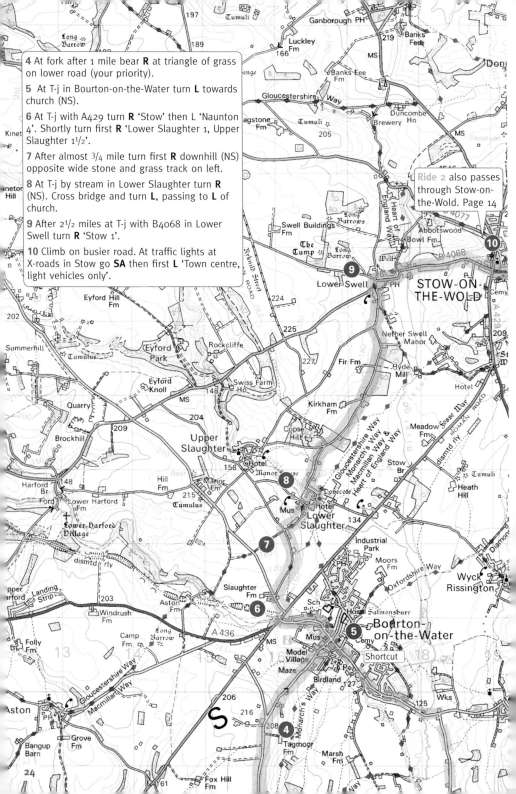

4 At fork after 1 mile bear **R** at triangle of grass on lower road (your priority).

5 At T-j in Bourton-on-the-Water turn **L** towards church (NS).

6 At T-j with A429 turn **R** 'Stow' then L 'Naunton 4'. Shortly turn first **R** 'Lower Slaughter 1, Upper Slaughter 1½'.

7 After almost ¾ mile turn first **R** downhill (NS) opposite wide stone and grass track on left.

8 At T-j by stream in Lower Slaughter turn **R** (NS). Cross bridge and turn **L**, passing to **L** of church.

9 After 2½ miles at T-j with B4068 in Lower Swell turn **R** 'Stow 1'.

10 Climb on busier road. At traffic lights at X-roads in Stow go **SA** then first **L** 'Town centre, light vehicles only'.

Ride 2 also passes through Stow-on-the-Wold. Page 14

24

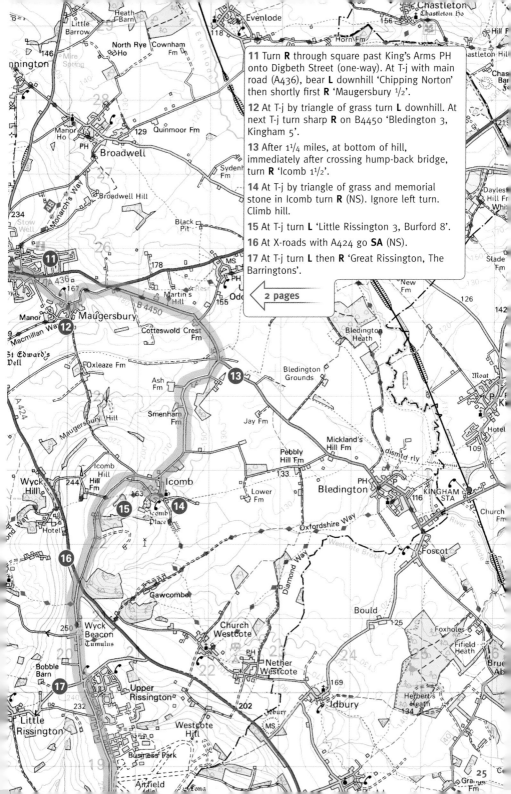

11 Turn **R** through square past King's Arms PH onto Digbeth Street (one-way). At T-j with main road (A436), bear **L** downhill 'Chipping Norton' then shortly first **R** 'Maugersbury ½'.

12 At T-j by triangle of grass turn **L** downhill. At next T-j turn sharp **R** on B4450 'Bledington 3, Kingham 5'.

13 After 1¼ miles, at bottom of hill, immediately after crossing hump-back bridge, turn **R** 'Icomb 1½'.

14 At T-j by triangle of grass and memorial stone in Icomb turn **R** (NS). Ignore left turn. Climb hill.

15 At T-j turn **L** 'Little Rissington 3, Burford 8'.

16 At X-roads with A424 go **SA** (NS).

17 At T-j turn **L** then **R** 'Great Rissington, The Barringtons'.

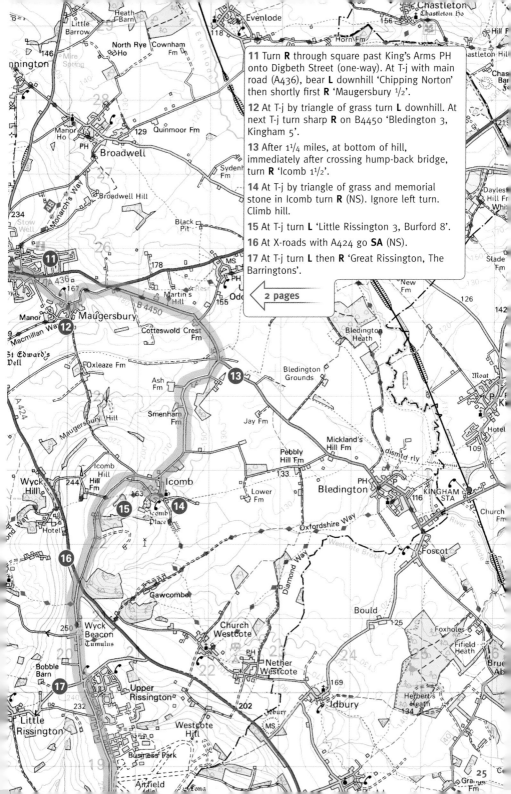

2 pages

Burford west to Northleach

Burford is justifiably popular with cyclists - not only is it a very attractive town with plenty of cafés and pubs but it is also blessed with quiet exits to east and west, soon linking to networks of delightful lanes spreading in every direction through the Cotswolds, avoiding the busy and unpleasant A roads. On this ride the lovely River Windrush and its tributary Sherborne

Brook are followed west as far as the handsome town of Northleach. South from here the route crosses the Salt Way, still marked on maps if you look hard enough. This route started at the salt mines in Droitwich and having

climbed up onto the Cotswold escarpment near Winchcombe (on Salter's Hill) took the easiest gradients to reach the Thames at Lechlade. The route joins the Coln Valley, passing through the pretty hamlets of Coln St Dennis and Coln Rogers then the larger villages of Ablington and Bibury, one of the top honeypots of the Cotswolds. Beyond Hatherop the ride briefly uses Akeman Street, one of the many such roads that radiated out from the important Roman settlement at Cirencester (Corinium) which became the second largest Roman town in Britain. Akeman Street connected Cirencester to Verulamium (near St Albans). After crossing the River Leach, climb across the open pasture land bounded by dry stone walls either side of Westwell before dropping back down into Burford.

Overview
On-road ● 29 miles / 47 kilometres ● Easy / Moderate

Start
Tolsey Museum, High Street, Burford

Parking
Free long-stay car park on Church Lane signposted off to the right near the bottom of the High Street

Busy roads
A361 / A424 through Burford

Terrain
Gently undulating - the whole route lies between 100 - 200m (330 - 660ft)

Nearest railway
Shipton-under-Wychwood

Other rides nearby

Refreshments
Burford
Lots of choice

Great Barrington
Fox Inn
T: 01451 844385

Sherborne
Sherborne Village Shop Tearoom

Northleach
Lots of choice

Bibury
Swan Hotel
T: 01285 740695
Catherine Wheel
T: 01285 740250

Coln St Aldwyns
New Inn
T: 01285 750651

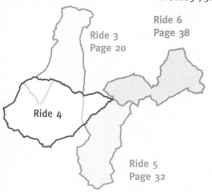

Ride 3
Page 20

Ride 6
Page 38

Ride 4

Ride 5
Page 32

Map pages

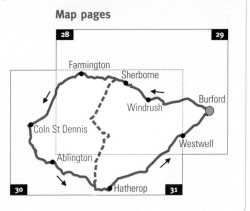

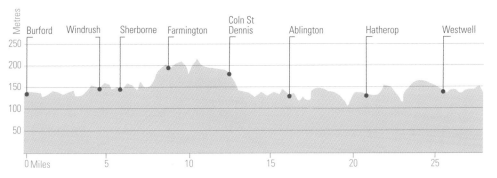

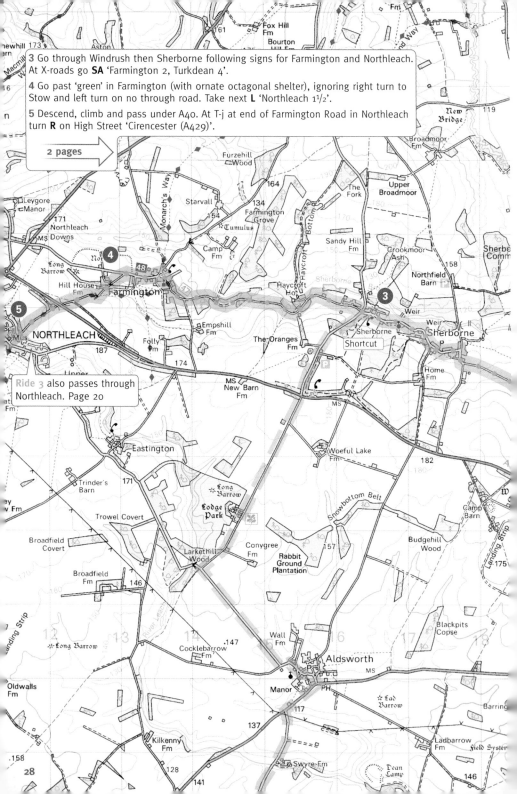

3 Go through Windrush then Sherborne following signs for Farmington and Northleach. At X-roads go **SA** 'Farmington 2, Turkdean 4'.

4 Go past 'green' in Farmington (with ornate octagonal shelter), ignoring right turn to Stow and left turn on no through road. Take next **L** 'Northleach 1½'.

5 Descend, climb and pass under A40. At T-j at end of Farmington Road in Northleach turn **R** on High Street 'Cirencester (A429)'.

2 pages

Ride 3 also passes through Northleach. Page 20

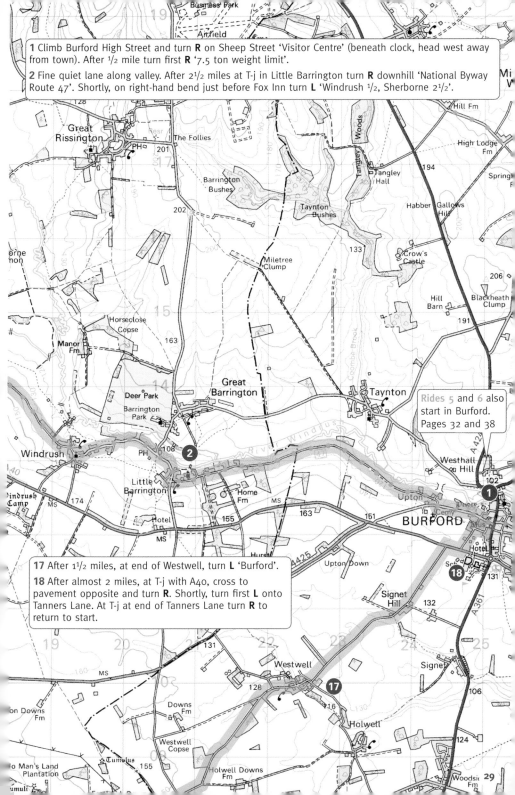

1 Climb Burford High Street and turn **R** on Sheep Street 'Visitor Centre' (beneath clock, head west away from town). After ½ mile turn first **R** '7.5 ton weight limit'.

2 Fine quiet lane along valley. After 2½ miles at T-j in Little Barrington turn **R** downhill 'National Byway Route 47'. Shortly, on right-hand bend just before Fox Inn turn **L** 'Windrush ½, Sherborne 2½'.

Rides 5 and 6 also start in Burford. Pages 32 and 38.

17 After 1½ miles, at end of Westwell, turn **L** 'Burford'.

18 After almost 2 miles, at T-j with A40, cross to pavement opposite and turn **R**. Shortly, turn first **L** onto Tanners Lane. At T-j at end of Tanners Lane turn **R** to return to start.

29

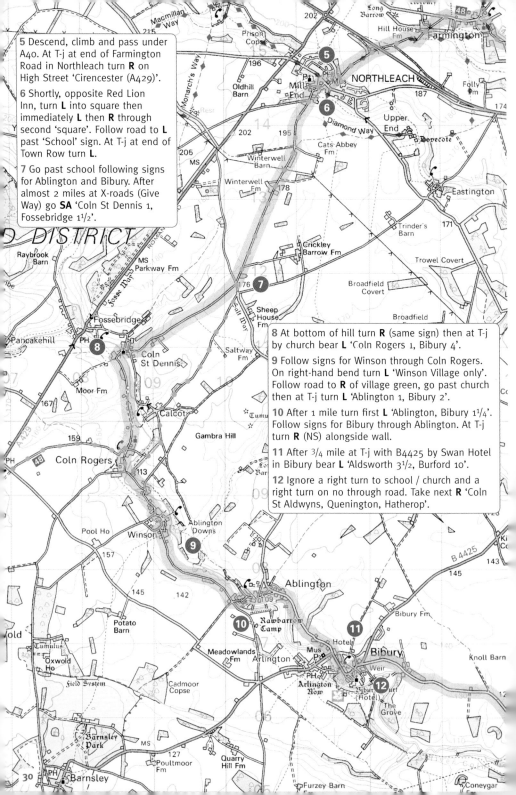

5 Descend, climb and pass under A40. At T-j at end of Farmington Road in Northleach turn **R** on High Street 'Cirencester (A429)'.

6 Shortly, opposite Red Lion Inn, turn **L** into square then immediately **L** then **R** through second 'square'. Follow road to **L** past 'School' sign. At T-j at end of Town Row turn **L**.

7 Go past school following signs for Ablington and Bibury. After almost 2 miles at X-roads (Give Way) go **SA** 'Coln St Dennis 1, Fossebridge 1½'.

8 At bottom of hill turn **R** (same sign) then at T-j by church bear **L** 'Coln Rogers 1, Bibury 4'.

9 Follow signs for Winson through Coln Rogers. On right-hand bend turn **L** 'Winson Village only'. Follow road to **R** of village green, go past church then at T-j turn **L** 'Ablington 1, Bibury 2'.

10 After 1 mile turn first **L** 'Ablington, Bibury 1¼'. Follow signs for Bibury through Ablington. At T-j turn **R** (NS) alongside wall.

11 After ¾ mile at T-j with B4425 by Swan Hotel in Bibury bear **L** 'Aldsworth 3½, Burford 10'.

12 Ignore a right turn to school / church and a right turn on no through road. Take next **R** 'Coln St Aldwyns, Quenington, Hatherop'.

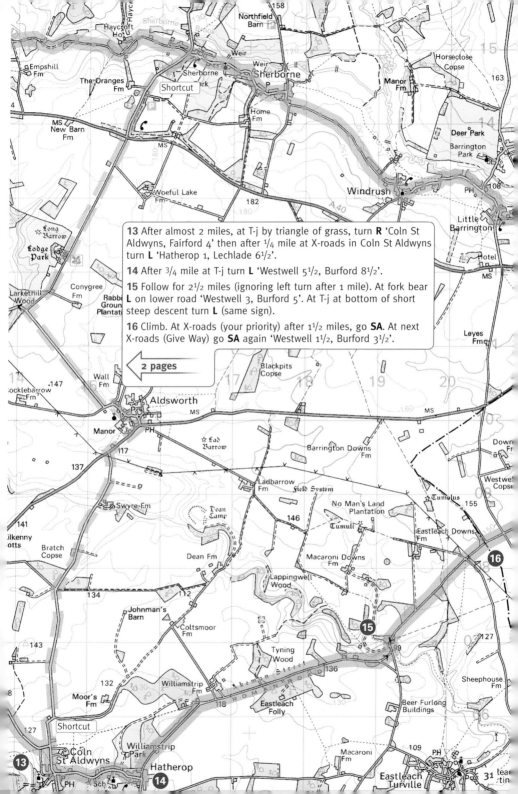

13 After almost 2 miles, at T-j by triangle of grass, turn **R** 'Coln St Aldwyns, Fairford 4' then after ¼ mile at X-roads in Coln St Aldwyns turn **L** 'Hatherop 1, Lechlade 6½'.

14 After ¾ mile at T-j turn **L** 'Westwell 5½, Burford 8½'.

15 Follow for 2½ miles (ignoring left turn after 1 mile). At fork bear **L** on lower road 'Westwell 3, Burford 5'. At T-j at bottom of short steep descent turn **L** (same sign).

16 Climb. At X-roads (your priority) after 1½ miles, go **SA**. At next X-roads (Give Way) go **SA** again 'Westwell 1½, Burford 3½'.

2 pages

South from Burford to the Thames at Lechlade

Prosperity came to Burford through trade in wool and cloth, work in the stone quarries nearby and the manufacture of saddlery. Stone from the area was used in the construction of Blenheim Palace and many buildings in Oxford. Burford's great coaching days date from the times of the turnpike roads: providing for the feeding of travellers and their horses was a considerable trade. Moving from horses to bicycles, many of the rides in this book explore the valleys formed by the River Thames and its many tributaries, three of which, the Evenlode, the Windrush and the Coln, drain much of the Cotswolds,

flowing southeast to join the Thames. This ride follows the River Windrush east out of Burford, crossing the A40 at the same point as the old Roman Road of Akeman Street on its course east from Cirencester to St Albans. On your way south from Langford

you may wish to divert to visit Kelmscott. This Elizabethan Manor was the country home of William Morris, craftsman, socialist and designer, for 25 years from 1871 until his death in 1896. The Thames is joined at Lechlade, which was for many centuries the upper navigable limit of the river. It is at this point its size increases substantially with the waters of the River Coln, River Leach and River Cole. Cotswold stone was transported by barge from here down to Oxford and London. Lechlade has a fine array of buildings dating back to the 17th and 18th centuries. North from Lechlade you have myriad lane options to take you back into the Windrush valley and a return to the delights of Burford.

Overview
On-road ● 29 miles / 47 kilometres ● Easy

Start
Tolsey Museum, High Street, Burford

Parking
Free long-stay car park on Church Lane signposted off to the right near the bottom of the High Street

Busy roads
A417 / A361 through Lechlade to ⓮

Terrain
Gently undulating with no major hills

Nearest railway
Ascott-under-Wychwood

Refreshments

Burford
Lots of choice

Swinbrook
Swan Inn
T: 01993 823339

Shilton
Rose & Crown PH
T: 01993 842280

Langford
Bell Inn
T: 01367 860249

Kelmscott
Plough Inn
T: 01367 253543

Lechlade
Lots of choice

Southrop
Swan PH
T: 01367 850205

Eastleach
Victoria Inn
T: 01367 850277

Great Barrington
Fox Inn
T: 01451 844385

Map pages

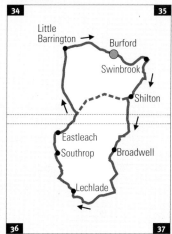

Other rides nearby

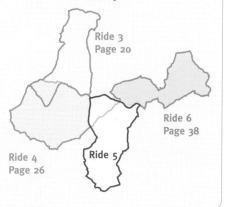

Ride 3
Page 20

Ride 6
Page 38

Ride 4
Page 26

Ride 5

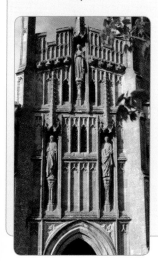

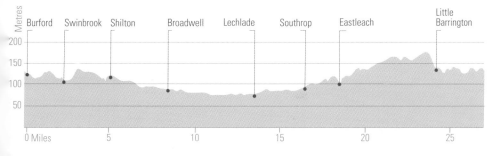

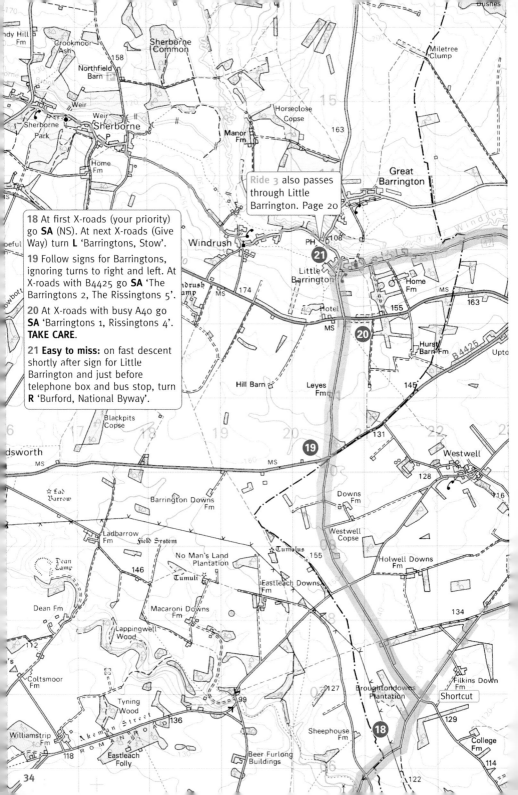

18 At first X-roads (your priority) go **SA** (NS). At next X-roads (Give Way) turn **L** 'Barringtons, Stow'.

19 Follow signs for Barringtons, ignoring turns to right and left. At X-roads with B4425 go **SA** 'The Barringtons 2, The Rissingtons 5'.

20 At X-roads with busy A40 go **SA** 'Barringtons 1, Rissingtons 4'. **TAKE CARE.**

21 Easy to miss: on fast descent shortly after sign for Little Barrington and just before telephone box and bus stop, turn **R** 'Burford, National Byway'.

Ride 3 also passes through Little Barrington. Page 20

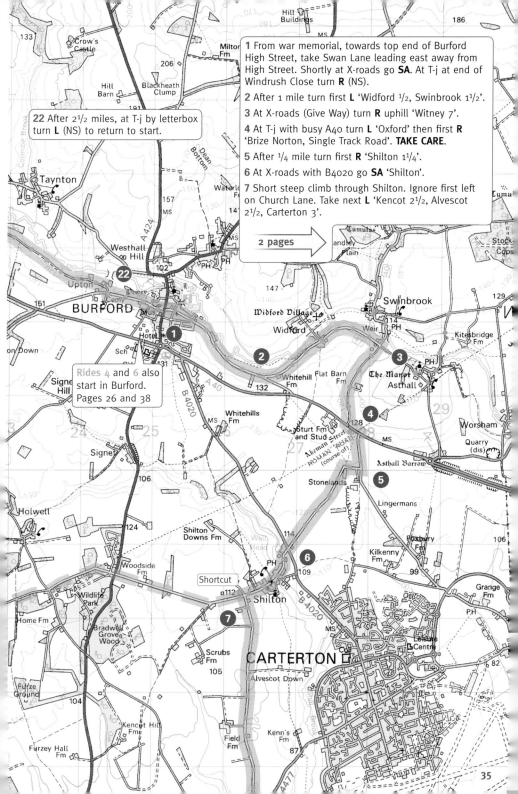

1 From war memorial, towards top end of Burford High Street, take Swan Lane leading east away from High Street. Shortly at X-roads go **SA**. At T-j at end of Windrush Close turn **R** (NS).

2 After 1 mile turn first **L** 'Widford ½, Swinbrook 1½'.

3 At X-roads (Give Way) turn **R** uphill 'Witney 7'.

4 At T-j with busy A40 turn **L** 'Oxford' then first **R** 'Brize Norton, Single Track Road'. **TAKE CARE.**

5 After ¼ mile turn first **R** 'Shilton 1¼'.

6 At X-roads with B4020 go **SA** 'Shilton'.

7 Short steep climb through Shilton. Ignore first left on Church Lane. Take next **L** 'Kencot 2½, Alvescot 2½, Carterton 3'.

22 After 2½ miles, at T-j by letterbox turn **L** (NS) to return to start.

2 pages

Rides 4 and 6 also start in Burford. Pages 26 and 38

Shortcut

35

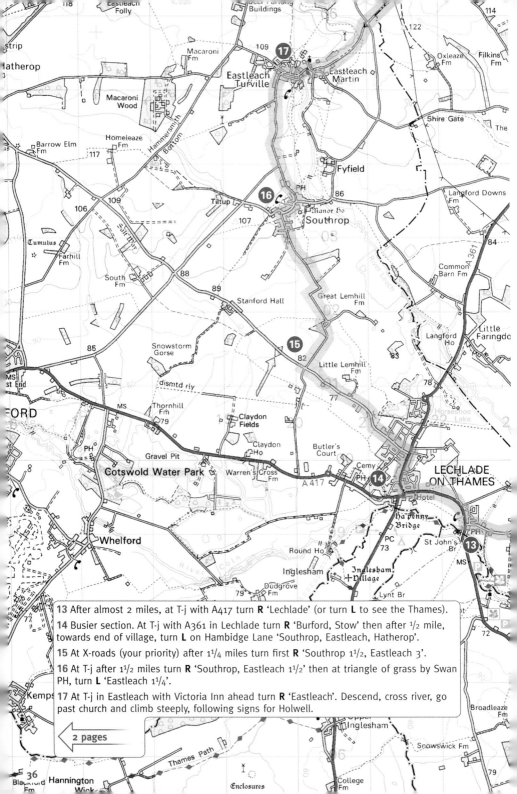

13 After almost 2 miles, at T-j with A417 turn **R** 'Lechlade' (or turn **L** to see the Thames).

14 Busier section. At T-j with A361 in Lechlade turn **R** 'Burford, Stow' then after ¹/₂ mile, towards end of village, turn **L** on Hambidge Lane 'Southrop, Eastleach, Hatherop'.

15 At X-roads (your priority) after 1¹/₄ miles turn first **R** 'Southrop 1¹/₂, Eastleach 3'.

16 At T-j after 1¹/₂ miles turn **R** 'Southrop, Eastleach 1¹/₂' then at triangle of grass by Swan PH, turn **L** 'Eastleach 1¹/₄'.

17 At T-j in Eastleach with Victoria Inn ahead turn **R** 'Eastleach'. Descend, cross river, go past church and climb steeply, following signs for Holwell.

2 pages

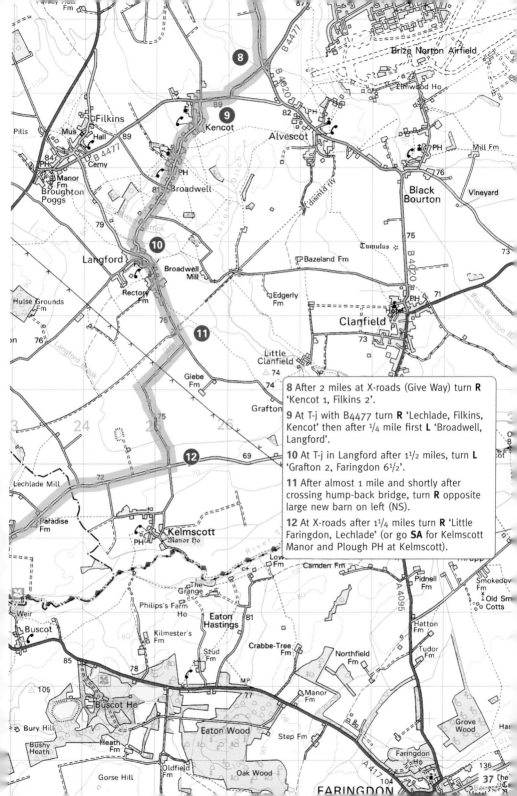

8 After 2 miles at X-roads (Give Way) turn **R** 'Kencot 1, Filkins 2'.

9 At T-j with B4477 turn **R** 'Lechlade, Filkins, Kencot' then after ¼ mile first **L** 'Broadwell, Langford'.

10 At T-j in Langford after 1½ miles, turn **L** 'Grafton 2, Faringdon 6½'.

11 After almost 1 mile and shortly after crossing hump-back bridge, turn **R** opposite large new barn on left (NS).

12 At X-roads after 1¼ miles turn **R** 'Little Faringdon, Lechlade' (or go **SA** for Kelmscott Manor and Plough PH at Kelmscott).

East from Burford through Wychwood Forest to Charlbury

The last of the three rides starting from Burford strikes northeast through the remnants of Wychwood Forest. This has been a royal forest since Saxon times, with a royal hunting lodge at Woodstock. It used to extend from the Glyme valley south to the Thames and from Taynton in the west to the Cherwell valley in the east. Estates at Blenheim, Cornbury, Ditchley and Eynsham were carved out of it. The remaining small triangle of woodland cloaks the higher

ground between the valleys formed by two of the principal tributaries of the Thames: the River Windrush, which passes through Burford, and the River Evenlode which passes beneath Charlbury. Both join old Father Thames to the west of Oxford. Charlbury's one-way system means it is best to walk your bike through the churchyard to get to the centre of town. A somewhat circuitous route avoids the busy roads around Witney to take you to Minster Lovell. It is worth diverting a few yards off the route to visit the

ruins of Minster Lovell Hall near to the church to the east of the village. The splendid 15th-century manor house has been a ruin since 1747 but its setting on the banks of the River Windrush is exceptional. Although you have dropped down into the Windrush valley there is one last climb to tackle to avoid busier roads, taking you up to Asthall Leigh. The manor houses at Asthall and Widford are two striking architectural delights as you proceed east back to Burford.

Overview

On-road ● 30 miles / 48 kilometres ● Easy / Moderate

Start
Tolsey Museum, High Street, Burford

Parking
Free long-stay car park on Church Lane signposted off to the right near the bottom of the High Street

Busy roads
● A361 / A424 through Burford ❶

● B4437 west of Charlbury ⓫

● B4022 south of Charlbury ⓮

Terrain
Gently undulating with one longer climb (330ft / 100m) at the start north from Burford

Nearest railway
Charlbury

Refreshments
Burford
Lots of choice

Leafield
Fox Inn
T: 01993 878647

Charlbury
Lots of choice

North Leigh
Masons Arms PH
T: 01993 882005

New Yatt
Woodman Inn
T: 01993 881790
Saddlers Arms PH
T: 01993 868115

Minster Lovell
Old Swan PH
T: 01993 774441

Asthall
Maytime Inn
T: 01993 822068

Map pages

42 · Charlbury · 43
Fawler
Leafield
Delly End
Taynton · Fordwells · North Leigh
Burford
Asthall · Minster Lovell
40 · 41

Other rides nearby

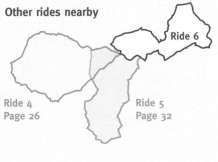

Ride 6

Ride 4
Page 26

Ride 5
Page 32

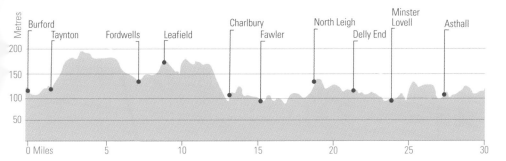

Metres

Burford
Taynton
Fordwells
Leafield
Charlbury
Fawler
North Leigh
Delly End
Minster Lovell
Asthall

200
150
100
50

0 Miles · 5 · 10 · 15 · 20 · 25 · 30

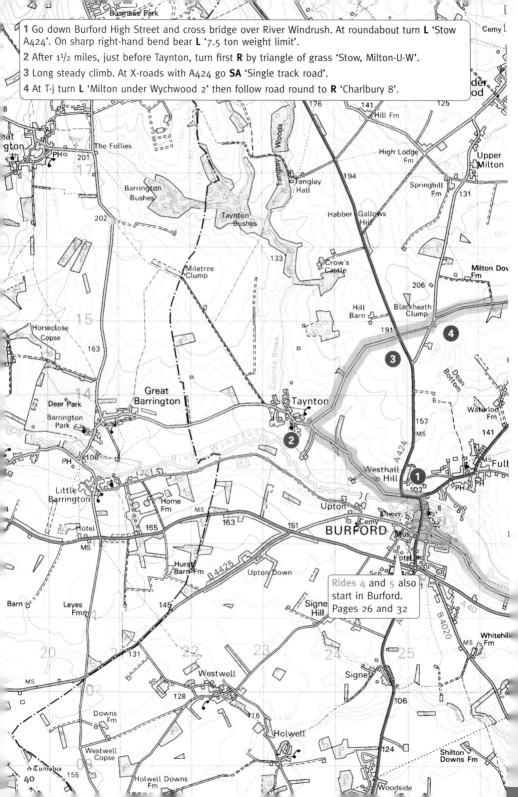

1 Go down Burford High Street and cross bridge over River Windrush. At roundabout turn **L** 'Stow A424'. On sharp right-hand bend bear **L** '7.5 ton weight limit'.

2 After 1½ miles, just before Taynton, turn first **R** by triangle of grass 'Stow, Milton-U-W'.

3 Long steady climb. At X-roads with A424 go **SA** 'Single track road'.

4 At T-j turn **L** 'Milton under Wychwood 2' then follow road round to **R** 'Charlbury 8'.

Rides 4 and 5 also start in Burford. Pages 26 and 32

40

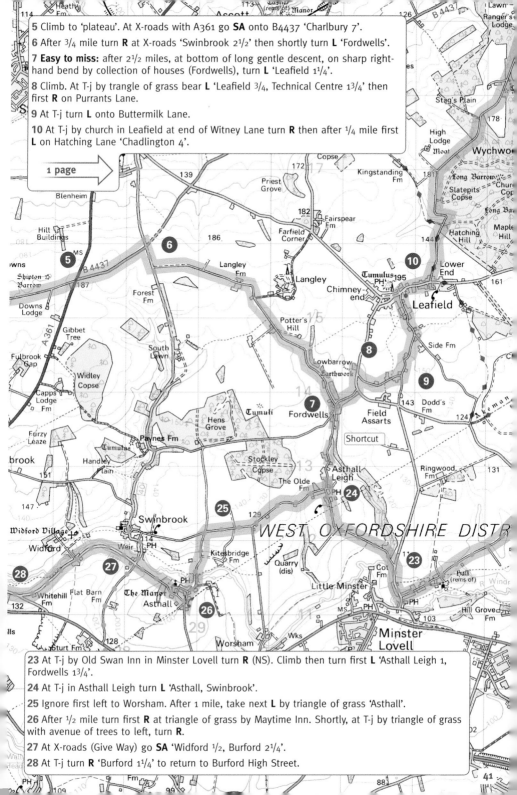

5 Climb to 'plateau'. At X-roads with A361 go **SA** onto B4437 'Charlbury 7'.

6 After 3/4 mile turn **R** at X-roads 'Swinbrook 2½' then shortly turn **L** 'Fordwells'.

7 Easy to miss: after 2½ miles, at bottom of long gentle descent, on sharp right-hand bend by collection of houses (Fordwells), turn **L** 'Leafield 1¼'.

8 Climb. At T-j by trangle of grass bear **L** 'Leafield 3/4, Technical Centre 1¾' then first **R** on Purrants Lane.

9 At T-j turn **L** onto Buttermilk Lane.

10 At T-j by church in Leafield at end of Witney Lane turn **R** then after ¼ mile first **L** on Hatching Lane 'Chadlington 4'.

1 page

23 At T-j by Old Swan Inn in Minster Lovell turn **R** (NS). Climb then turn first **L** 'Asthall Leigh 1, Fordwells 1¾'.

24 At T-j in Asthall Leigh turn **L** 'Asthall, Swinbrook'.

25 Ignore first left to Worsham. After 1 mile, take next **L** by triangle of grass 'Asthall'.

26 After ½ mile turn first **R** at triangle of grass by Maytime Inn. Shortly, at T-j by triangle of grass with avenue of trees to left, turn **R**.

27 At X-roads (Give Way) go **SA** 'Widford ½, Burford 2¼'.

28 At T-j turn **R** 'Burford 1¼' to return to Burford High Street.

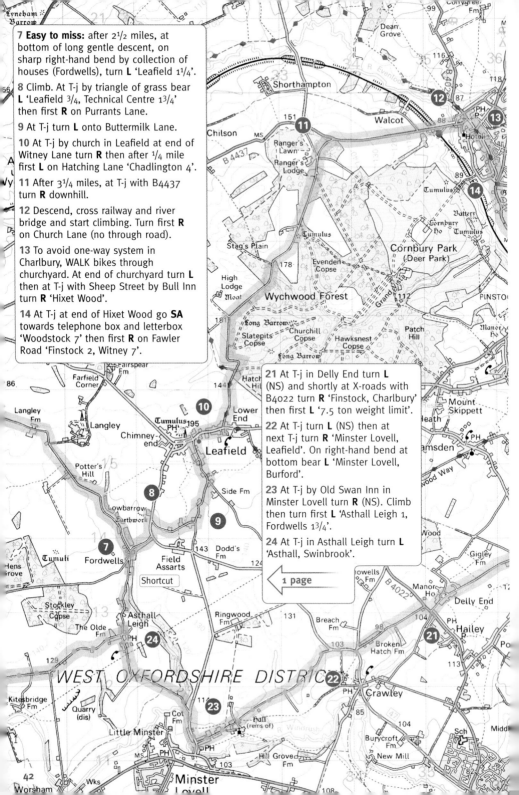

7 Easy to miss: after 2½ miles, at bottom of long gentle descent, on sharp right-hand bend by collection of houses (Fordwells), turn **L** 'Leafield 1¼'.

8 Climb. At T-j by triangle of grass bear **L** 'Leafield ¾, Technical Centre 1¾' then first **R** on Purrants Lane.

9 At T-j turn **L** onto Buttermilk Lane.

10 At T-j by church in Leafield at end of Witney Lane turn **R** then after ¼ mile first **L** on Hatching Lane 'Chadlington 4'.

11 After 3¼ miles, at T-j with B4437 turn **R** downhill.

12 Descend, cross railway and river bridge and start climbing. Turn first **R** on Church Lane (no through road).

13 To avoid one-way system in Charlbury, WALK bikes through churchyard. At end of churchyard turn **L** then at T-j with Sheep Street by Bull Inn turn **R** 'Hixet Wood'.

14 At T-j at end of Hixet Wood go **SA** towards telephone box and letterbox 'Woodstock 7' then first **R** on Fawler Road 'Finstock 2, Witney 7'.

21 At T-j in Delly End turn **L** (NS) and shortly at X-roads with B4022 turn **R** 'Finstock, Charlbury' then first **L** '7.5 ton weight limit'.

22 At T-j turn **L** (NS) then at next T-j turn **R** 'Minster Lovell, Leafield'. On right-hand bend at bottom bear **L** 'Minster Lovell, Burford'.

23 At T-j by Old Swan Inn in Minster Lovell turn **R** (NS). Climb then turn first **L** 'Asthall Leigh 1, Fordwells 1¾'.

24 At T-j in Asthall Leigh turn **L** 'Asthall, Swinbrook'.

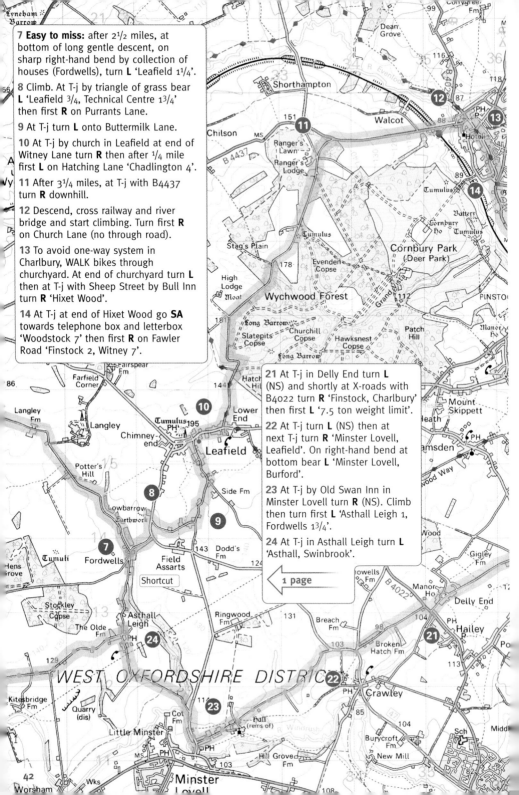
← 1 page

42

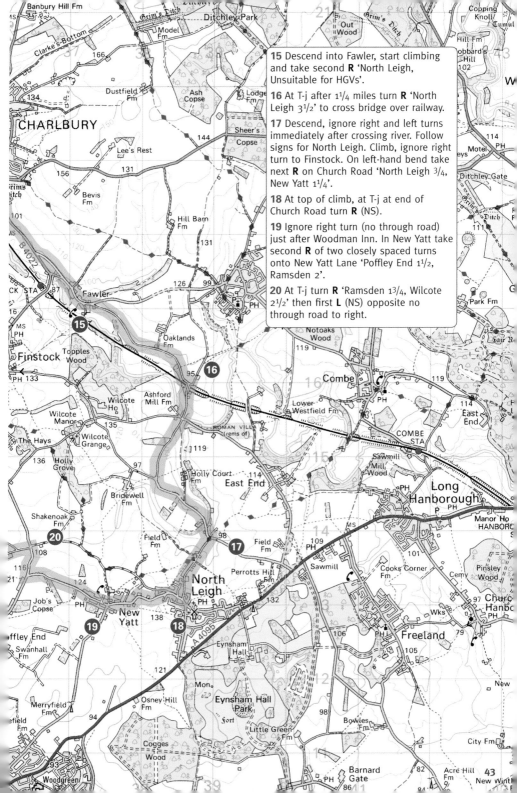

15 Descend into Fawler, start climbing and take second **R** 'North Leigh, Unsuitable for HGVs'.

16 At T-j after 1¼ miles turn **R** 'North Leigh 3½' to cross bridge over railway.

17 Descend, ignore right and left turns immediately after crossing river. Follow signs for North Leigh. Climb, ignore right turn to Finstock. On left-hand bend take next **R** on Church Road 'North Leigh ¾, New Yatt 1¼'.

18 At top of climb, at T-j at end of Church Road turn **R** (NS).

19 Ignore right turn (no through road) just after Woodman Inn. In New Yatt take second **R** of two closely spaced turns onto New Yatt Lane 'Poffley End 1½, Ramsden 2'.

20 At T-j turn **R** 'Ramsden 1¾, Wilcote 2½' then first **L** (NS) opposite no through road to right.

Woodstock, the Tews & the Cherwell Valley

motors', and passing through Radford and Cleveley, has a timeless feel to it, as though you have stepped into a different age. You are abruptly woken from the dream with a short busy section on the B4022 through Enstone before disappearing once again onto delightful little roads through to the pretty village of Little Tew. It is worth diverting less than ¹/₂ mile off the main route to see the lovely buildings, some of which are thatched, in the village of Great Tew. It was largely built as a model village by the 19th-century landscape gardener John Loudon and it is because of him that there are so many evergreen trees in the surrounding area. There is also a café and a pub here. East from here the ride drops down into the valley of the River Cherwell, one of the longest tributaries of the River Thames, running parallel with the Oxford Canal well to the north of Banbury. The traffic-free section of National Cycle Network Route 5 is rejoined southwest of Rousham and offers a gentle, stress-free entrance back into Woodstock.

Woodstock originally grew in importance as a base for royalty to house their retinues while hunting in the nearby Wychwood Forest. The town is dominated by Blenheim Palace, built for the Duke of Marlborough in the early 18th century. A traffic-free section of National Cycle Network Route 5 neatly links the library in the centre of Woodstock with a network of lanes that avoids the busy A44 altogether. The River Glyme is crossed just south of Wootton as you head northwest from Woodstock. The lane you follow after Kiddington, enticingly signposted 'Unsuitable for

Overview
On-road ● 28 miles / 45 kilometres ● Easy / Moderate

Start
Library car park, Woodstock

Parking
As above

Busy roads
B4022 in Enstone **10** to **11**

Terrain
Undulating

Nearest railway
Charlbury

Refreshments
Woodstock
Lots of choice

Wootton
Killingworth Castle Inn
T: 01993 811401
Kings Head Inn
T: 01993 811340

Enstone
Harrow Inn
T: 01608 677262
Crown Inn
T: 01608 677366

Duns Tew
White Horse PH
T: 01869 340272

Steeple Aston
White Lion PH
T: 01869 340307
Red Lion PH
T: 01869 340225

Other rides nearby

Ride 1
Page 8

Ride 7

Map pages

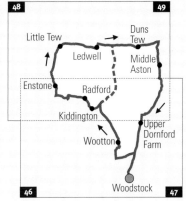

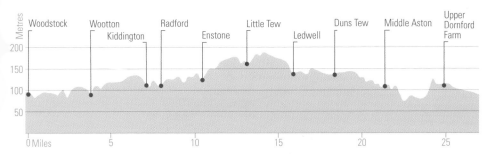

45

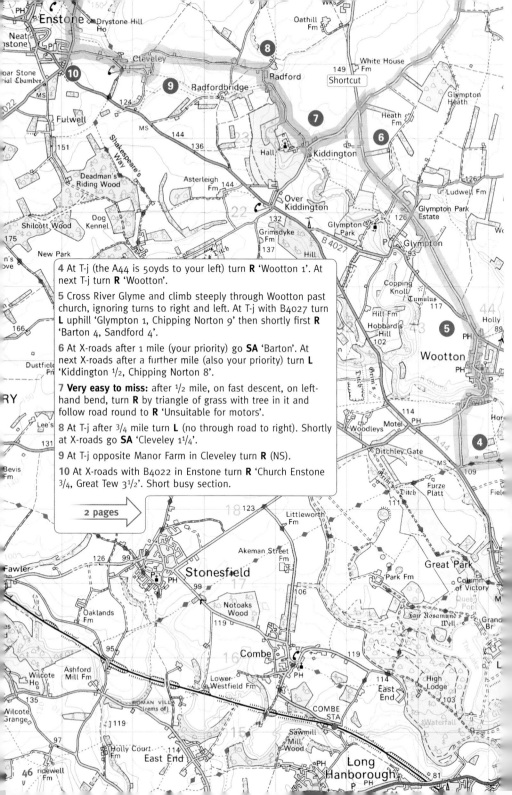

4 At T-j (the A44 is 50yds to your left) turn **R** 'Wootton 1'. At next T-j turn **R** 'Wootton'.

5 Cross River Glyme and climb steeply through Wootton past church, ignoring turns to right and left. At T-j with B4027 turn **L** uphill 'Glympton 1, Chipping Norton 9' then shortly first **R** 'Barton 4, Sandford 4'.

6 At X-roads after 1 mile (your priority) go **SA** 'Barton'. At next X-roads after a further mile (also your priority) turn **L** 'Kiddington ¹/₂, Chipping Norton 8'.

7 Very easy to miss: after ¹/₂ mile, on fast descent, on left-hand bend, turn **R** by triangle of grass with tree in it and follow road round to **R** 'Unsuitable for motors'.

8 At T-j after ³/₄ mile turn **L** (no through road to right). Shortly at X-roads go **SA** 'Cleveley 1¹/₄'.

9 At T-j opposite Manor Farm in Cleveley turn **R** (NS).

10 At X-roads with B4022 in Enstone turn **R** 'Church Enstone ³/₄, Great Tew 3¹/₂'. Short busy section.

2 pages →

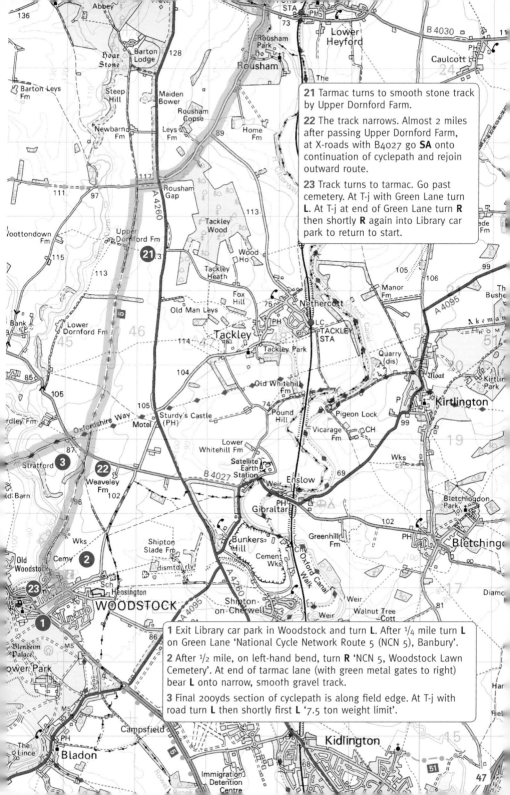

21 Tarmac turns to smooth stone track by Upper Dornford Farm.

22 The track narrows. Almost 2 miles after passing Upper Dornford Farm, at X-roads with B4027 go **SA** onto continuation of cyclepath and rejoin outward route.

23 Track turns to tarmac. Go past cemetery. At T-j with Green Lane turn **L**. At T-j at end of Green Lane turn **R** then shortly **R** again into Library car park to return to start.

1 Exit Library car park in Woodstock and turn **L**. After ¹/₄ mile turn **L** on Green Lane 'National Cycle Network Route 5 (NCN 5), Banbury'.

2 After ¹/₂ mile, on left-hand bend, turn **R** 'NCN 5, Woodstock Lawn Cemetery'. At end of tarmac lane (with green metal gates to right) bear **L** onto narrow, smooth gravel track.

3 Final 200yds section of cyclepath is along field edge. At T-j with road turn **L** then shortly first **L** '7.5 ton weight limit'.

47

6 At X-roads after 1 mile (your priority) go **SA** 'Barton'. At next X-roads after a further mile (also your priority) turn **L** 'Kiddington ½, Chipping Norton 8'.

7 Very easy to miss: after ½ mile, on fast descent, on left-hand bend, turn **R** by triangle of grass with tree in it and follow road round to **R** 'Unsuitable for motors'.

8 At T-j after ¾ mile turn **L** (no through road to right). Shortly at X-roads go **SA** 'Cleveley 1¼'.

9 At T-j opposite Manor Farm in Cleveley turn **R** (NS).

10 At X-roads with B4022 in Enstone turn **R** 'Church Enstone ¾, Great Tew 3½'. Short busy section.

11 Descend, climb then turn first **L** onto tiny lane 'Unsuitable for HGVs'. Shortly at T-j with B4030 turn **R** then **L** 'Little Tew'.

12 At T-j in Little Tew after 2½ miles turn **R** 'Great Tew 1¼'.

13 At X-roads with B4022 go **SA** 'Ledwell 1½, Duns Tew 4½'.

*After ¼ mile you may wish to turn first **L** to visit Great Tew. Return to this point.*

14 (Main route). At X-roads after 1¾ miles turn **L** 'Nether Worton 1, Barford 3, Duns Tew 2' then at bottom of hill turn first **R** 'Duns Tew 2'.

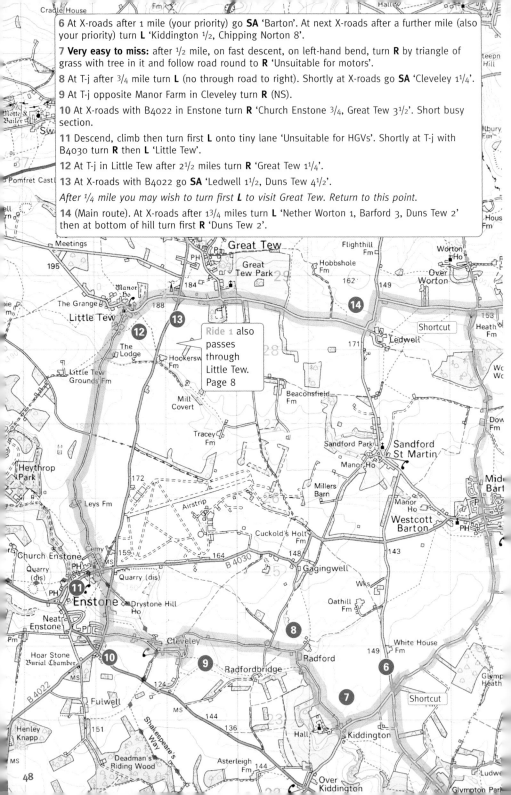

Ride 1 also passes through Little Tew. Page 8

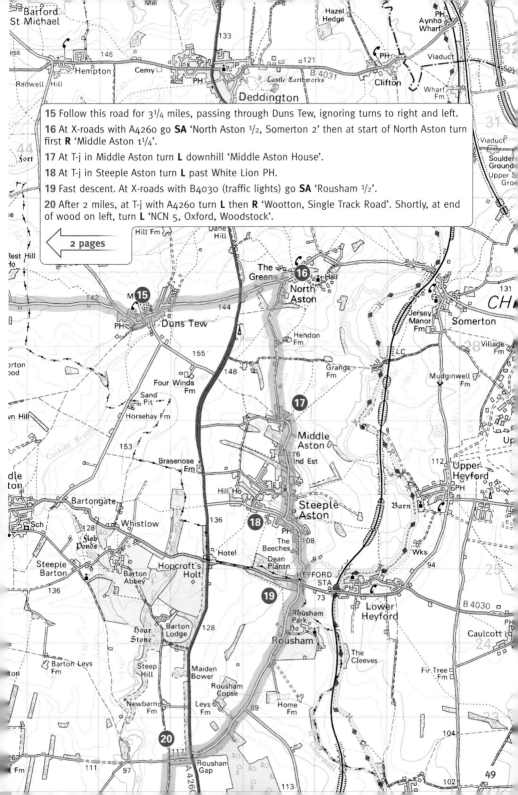

15 Follow this road for 3¼ miles, passing through Duns Tew, ignoring turns to right and left.

16 At X-roads with A4260 go **SA** 'North Aston ½, Somerton 2' then at start of North Aston turn first **R** 'Middle Aston 1¼'.

17 At T-j in Middle Aston turn **L** downhill 'Middle Aston House'.

18 At T-j in Steeple Aston turn **L** past White Lion PH.

19 Fast descent. At X-roads with B4030 (traffic lights) go **SA** 'Rousham ½'.

20 After 2 miles, at T-j with A4260 turn **L** then **R** 'Wootton, Single Track Road'. Shortly, at end of wood on left, turn **L** 'NCN 5, Oxford, Woodstock'.

2 pages

49

Exploring the Downs north & west of Lambourn

Lambourn and the Lambourn Valley are famous for their association with racehorses and there is a good chance you will see magnificent thoroughbreds galloping across the smooth grass

tracks running parallel with the roads. Leave Lambourn to the north, heading towards the Ridgeway and branching off the B4001 as soon as possible onto the minor lane past Seven Barrows to the top of Blowingstone Hill. As

you zoom down the hill after crossing the Ridgeway don't forget there is a Give Way sign at the bottom! Kingston Lisle is full of attractive thatched cottages and you may wish to divert off the route to see these or visit the pub. Cross the Vale of White Horse, named after the figure carved in chalk on the hillside beneath Uffington Castle. Pass through Uffington (location of Tom Brown's School Museum) and Shrivenham before turning south and heading for the hills, or more accurately the chalk escarpment, rising to 830ft (253m) on Charlbury Hill, above Hinton Parva. Briefly follow the course of the old Roman Road that used to link Cirencester to Silchester (near Basingstoke) as you drop down to the pretty village of Aldbourne. Tiny wooded lanes east of Preston lead east then north past Membury to set you up for a fine fast descent back to the start.

Overview

On-road ● 30 miles / 48 kilometres ● Moderate

Start
Crossroads in the centre of Lambourn

Parking
Car park on the B4000 south of village centre

Busy roads
● The B4001 north from Lambourn ❶ to ❷

● Southwest of Fox Hill towards Aldbourne ⑭ to ⑮

● The B4192 south of Aldbourne ⑯ to ⑰

● Near Membury, south of Lambourn ⑳

Terrain
Undulating with several long gentle hills. One steeper climb (up onto Marridge Hill) after Aldbourne

Nearest railway
Hungerford

Refreshments
Lambourn
Lots of choice

Kingston Lisle
Blowing Stone PH
T: 01367 820288

Uffington
Fox & Hounds PH
T: 01367 820680

Shrivenham
Lots of choice

Bishopstone
True Heart Inn
T: 01793 790080
Royal Oak PH
T: 01793 790481

Aldbourne
Crown PH
T: 01672 540214
Blue Boar PH
T: 01672 540237

Other rides nearby

Ride 8

Ride 9
Page 56

Map pages

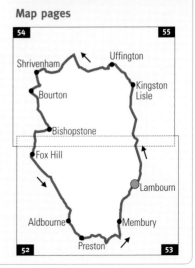

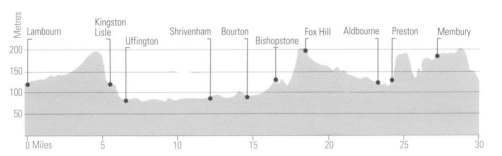

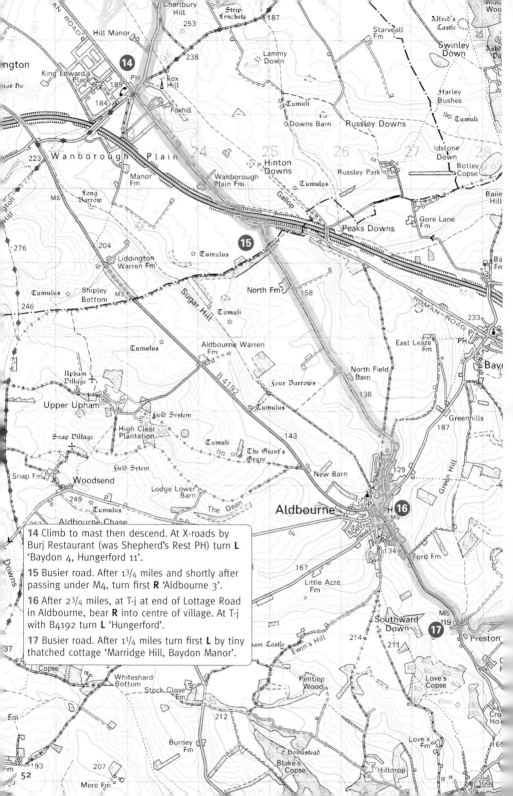

14 Climb to mast then descend. At X-roads by Burj Restaurant (was Shepherd's Rest PH) turn **L** 'Baydon 4, Hungerford 11'.

15 Busier road. After 1³/4 miles and shortly after passing under M4, turn first **R** 'Aldbourne 3'.

16 After 2³/4 miles, at T-j at end of Lottage Road in Aldbourne, bear **R** into centre of village. At T-j with B4192 turn **L** 'Hungerford'.

17 Busier road. After 1¹/4 miles turn first **L** by tiny thatched cottage 'Marridge Hill, Baydon Manor'.

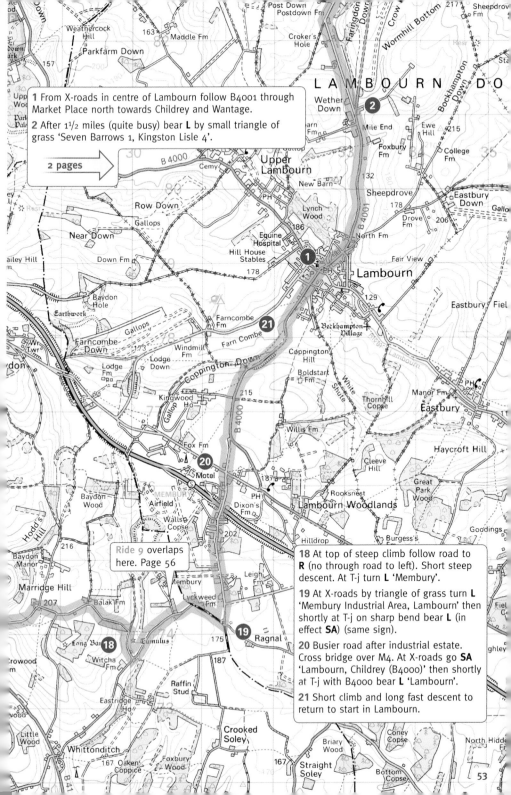

1 From X-roads in centre of Lambourn follow B4001 through Market Place north towards Childrey and Wantage.

2 After 1½ miles (quite busy) bear **L** by small triangle of grass 'Seven Barrows 1, Kingston Lisle 4'.

2 pages →

18 At top of steep climb follow road to **R** (no through road to left). Short steep descent. At T-j turn **L** 'Membury'.

19 At X-roads by triangle of grass turn **L** 'Membury Industrial Area, Lambourn' then shortly at T-j on sharp bend bear **L** (in effect **SA**) (same sign).

20 Busier road after industrial estate. Cross bridge over M4. At X-roads go **SA** 'Lambourn, Childrey (B4000)' then shortly at T-j with B4000 bear **L** 'Lambourn'.

21 Short climb and long fast descent to return to start in Lambourn.

Ride 9 overlaps here. Page 56

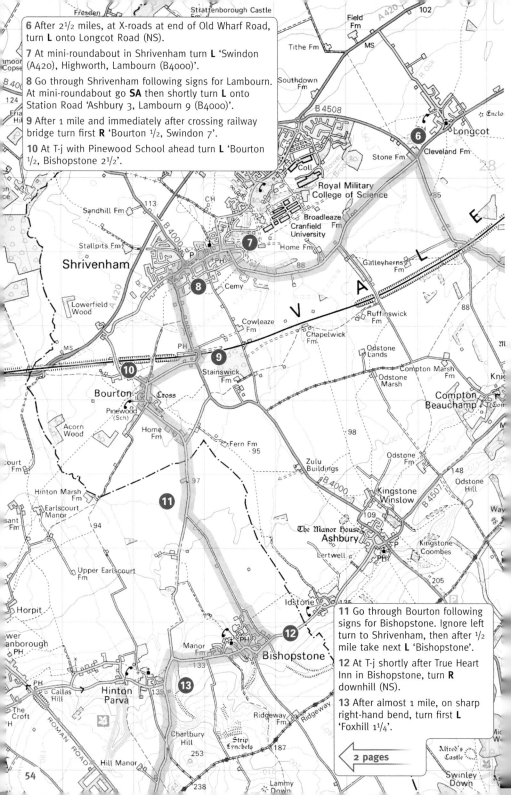

6 After 2¹/₂ miles, at X-roads at end of Old Wharf Road, turn **L** onto Longcot Road (NS).

7 At mini-roundabout in Shrivenham turn **L** 'Swindon (A420), Highworth, Lambourn (B4000)'.

8 Go through Shrivenham following signs for Lambourn. At mini-roundabout go **SA** then shortly turn **L** onto Station Road 'Ashbury 3, Lambourn 9 (B4000)'.

9 After 1 mile and immediately after crossing railway bridge turn first **R** 'Bourton ¹/₂, Swindon 7'.

10 At T-j with Pinewood School ahead turn **L** 'Bourton ¹/₂, Bishopstone 2¹/₂'.

11 Go through Bourton following signs for Bishopstone. Ignore left turn to Shrivenham, then after ¹/₂ mile take next **L** 'Bishopstone'.

12 At T-j shortly after True Heart Inn in Bishopstone, turn **R** downhill (NS).

13 After almost 1 mile, on sharp right-hand bend, turn first **L** 'Foxhill 1¹/₄'.

2 pages

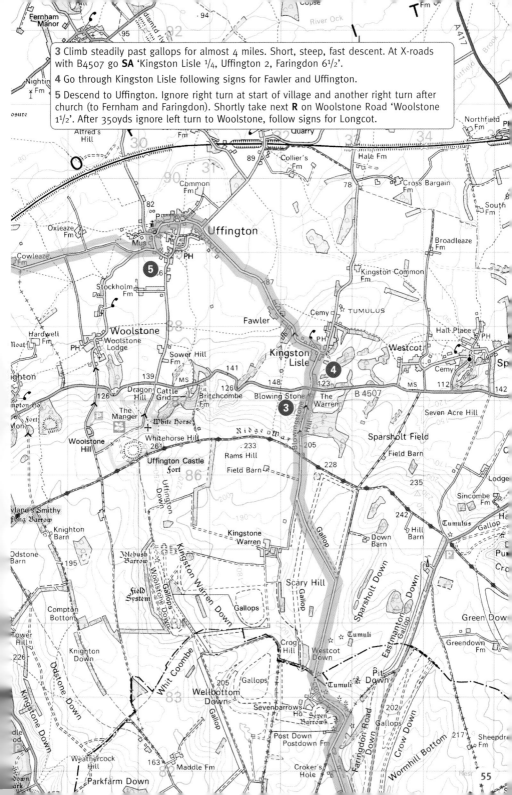

3 Climb steadily past gallops for almost 4 miles. Short, steep, fast descent. At X-roads with B4507 go **SA** 'Kingston Lisle ¼, Uffington 2, Faringdon 6½'.

4 Go through Kingston Lisle following signs for Fawler and Uffington.

5 Descend to Uffington. Ignore right turn at start of village and another right turn after church (to Fernham and Faringdon). Shortly take next **R** on Woolstone Road 'Woolstone 1½'. After 350yds ignore left turn to Woolstone, follow signs for Longcot.

From Hungerford to Marlborough along the Kennet Valley

The River Kennet is the linking theme for this ride, passing through the two handsome towns of Hungerford and Marlborough, both of which boast fine wide High Streets. Hungerford is set at the heart of an excellent network of quiet lanes ideal for exploration by bike with good exits to east and west from the very centre of town. The lane running west has been planted with an avenue of trees, first beech then horse chestnut. Cross the

canal at Little Bedwyn then make sure to stop at Great Bedwyn to read some of the bizarre inscriptions on the tombstones and stone tablets that adorn the old post office. For example:

'Here lies John Higgs / A famous man for killing pigs / For killing pigs was his delight / Both morning, afternoon and night', and many others. A circuitous route via Burbage, Wootton Rivers, a steep climb up onto Clench Common and a short section on the busy A345 enables you to approach Marlborough from the west on a quiet, at times traffic-free route dropping you right in the middle of its fine High Street and a wide choice of tea shops, cafés and pubs. A short section on a railway path gives the best and quietest escape eastwards from Marlborough to link with the road along the Kennet valley from Axford to the pretty village of Ramsbury. Climb up and away from the valley as you continue east before dropping back down into Hungerford to finish the ride.

Overview
On-road ● 37 miles / 59 kilometres ● Moderate

Start
Hungerford High Street by the clock tower

Parking
Long-stay car park on Church Street (off High Street)

Busy roads
● Almost 1 mile on A345 south of Marlborough (downhill) ⑫ to ⑬

● Short section on A4 and A338 back into Hungerford (30mph speed limit) ㉛ to ㉜

Terrain
Undulating. One steep climb north of Wootton Rivers towards Clench Common

Nearest railway
Hungerford

Refreshments
Hungerford
Lots of choice

Great Bedwyn
Three Tuns PH
T: 01672 870280
Cross Keys PH
T: 01672 870678

Stibb Green (Burbage)
Three Horseshoes
T: 01672 810324

Wootton Rivers
Royal Oak PH
T: 01672 810322

Marlborough
Lots of choice

Axford
Red Lion
T: 01672 520271

Ramsbury
Bell PH
T: 01672 520230
Crown & Anchor PH
T: 01672 520335

Other rides nearby

Ride 8
Page 50

Ride 10
Page 62

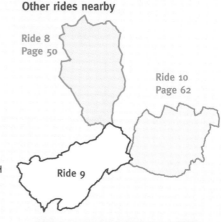

Ride 9

Map pages

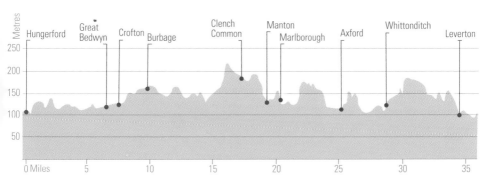

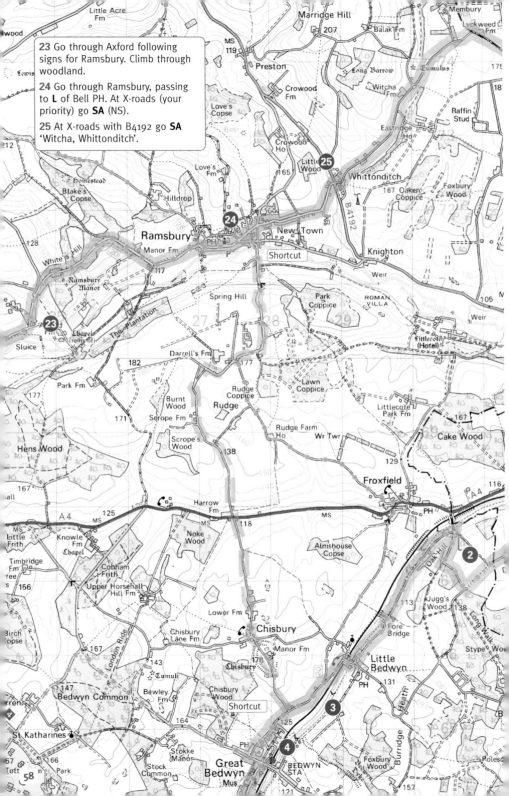

23 Go through Axford following signs for Ramsbury. Climb through woodland.

24 Go through Ramsbury, passing to **L** of Bell PH. At X-roads (your priority) go **SA** (NS).

25 At X-roads with B4192 go **SA** 'Witcha, Whittonditch'.

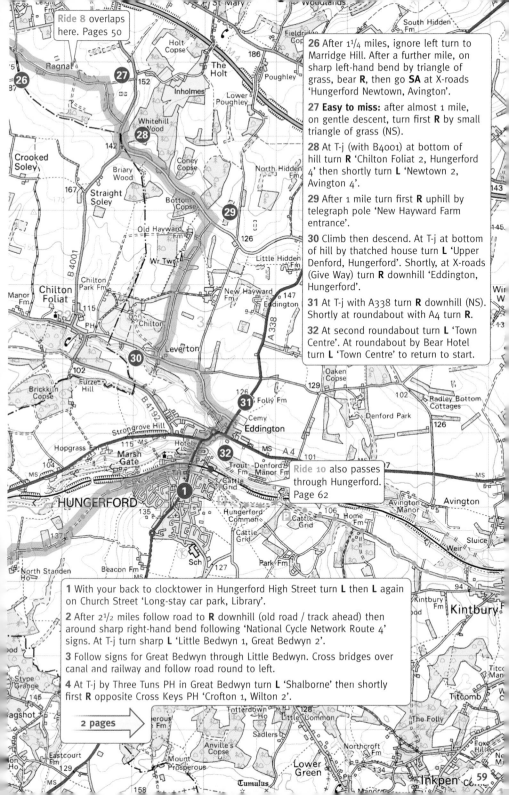

Ride 8 overlaps here. Pages 50

26 After 1¹/₄ miles, ignore left turn to Marridge Hill. After a further mile, on sharp left-hand bend by triangle of grass, bear **R**, then go **SA** at X-roads 'Hungerford Newtown, Avington'.

27 Easy to miss: after almost 1 mile, on gentle descent, turn first **R** by small triangle of grass (NS).

28 At T-j (with B4001) at bottom of hill turn **R** 'Chilton Foliat 2, Hungerford 4' then shortly turn **L** 'Newtown 2, Avington 4'.

29 After 1 mile turn first **R** uphill by telegraph pole 'New Hayward Farm entrance'.

30 Climb then descend. At T-j at bottom of hill by thatched house turn **L** 'Upper Denford, Hungerford'. Shortly, at X-roads (Give Way) turn **R** downhill 'Eddington, Hungerford'.

31 At T-j with A338 turn **R** downhill (NS). Shortly at roundabout with A4 turn **R**.

32 At second roundabout turn **L** 'Town Centre'. At roundabout by Bear Hotel turn **L** 'Town Centre' to return to start.

Ride 10 also passes through Hungerford. Page 62

1 With your back to clocktower in Hungerford High Street turn **L** then **L** again on Church Street 'Long-stay car park, Library'.

2 After 2¹/₂ miles follow road to **R** downhill (old road / track ahead) then around sharp right-hand bend following 'National Cycle Network Route 4' signs. At T-j turn sharp **L** 'Little Bedwyn 1, Great Bedwyn 2'.

3 Follow signs for Great Bedwyn through Little Bedwyn. Cross bridges over canal and railway and follow road round to left.

4 At T-j by Three Tuns PH in Great Bedwyn turn **L** 'Shalborne' then shortly first **R** opposite Cross Keys PH 'Crofton 1, Wilton 2'.

2 pages →

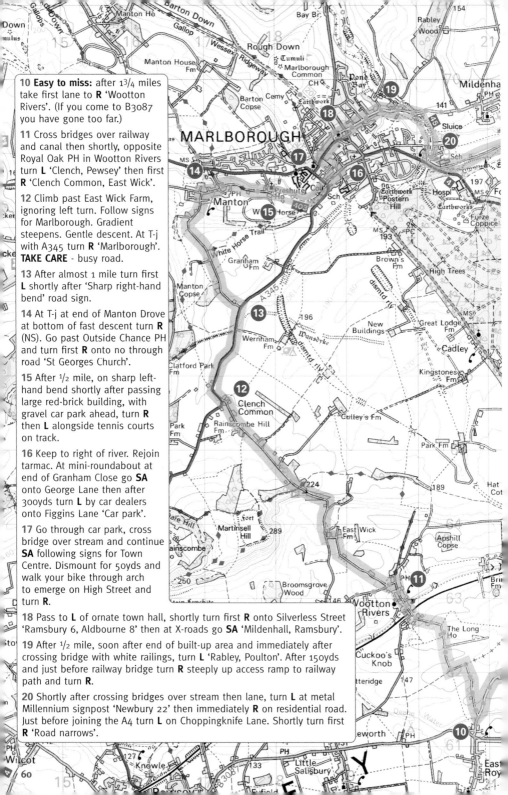

10 Easy to miss: after 1¾ miles take first lane to **R** 'Wootton Rivers'. (If you come to B3087 you have gone too far.)

11 Cross bridges over railway and canal then shortly, opposite Royal Oak PH in Wootton Rivers turn **L** 'Clench, Pewsey' then first **R** 'Clench Common, East Wick'.

12 Climb past East Wick Farm, ignoring left turn. Follow signs for Marlborough. Gradient steepens. Gentle descent. At T-j with A345 turn **R** 'Marlborough'. **TAKE CARE** - busy road.

13 After almost 1 mile turn first **L** shortly after 'Sharp right-hand bend' road sign.

14 At T-j at end of Manton Drove at bottom of fast descent turn **R** (NS). Go past Outside Chance PH and turn first **R** onto no through road 'St Georges Church'.

15 After ½ mile, on sharp left-hand bend shortly after passing large red-brick building, with gravel car park ahead, turn **R** then **L** alongside tennis courts on track.

16 Keep to right of river. Rejoin tarmac. At mini-roundabout at end of Granham Close go **SA** onto George Lane then after 300yds turn **L** by car dealers onto Figgins Lane 'Car park'.

17 Go through car park, cross bridge over stream and continue **SA** following signs for Town Centre. Dismount for 50yds and walk your bike through arch to emerge on High Street and turn **R**.

18 Pass to **L** of ornate town hall, shortly turn first **R** onto Silverless Street 'Ramsbury 6, Aldbourne 8' then at X-roads go **SA** 'Mildenhall, Ramsbury'.

19 After ½ mile, soon after end of built-up area and immediately after crossing bridge with white railings, turn **L** 'Rabley, Poulton'. After 150yds and just before railway bridge turn **R** steeply up access ramp to railway path and turn **R**.

20 Shortly after crossing bridges over stream then lane, turn **L** at metal Millennium signpost 'Newbury 22' then immediately **R** on residential road. Just before joining the A4 turn **L** on Choppingknife Lane. Shortly turn first **R** 'Road narrows'.

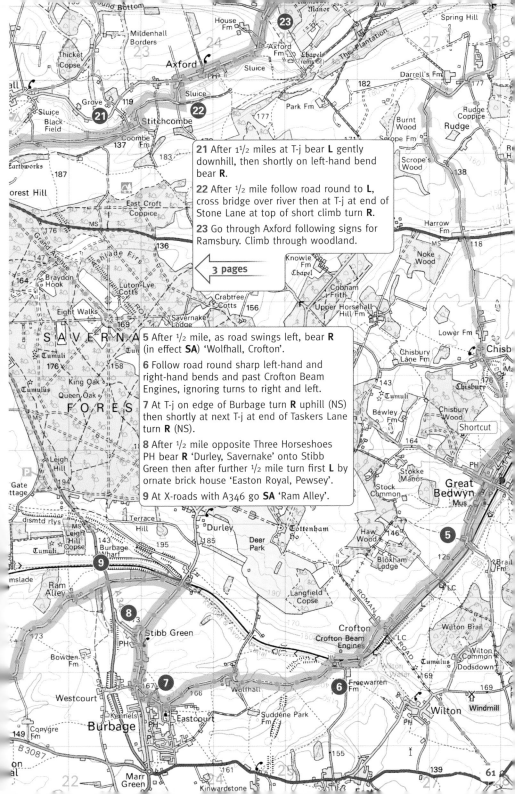

21 After 1½ miles at T-j bear **L** gently downhill, then shortly on left-hand bend bear **R**.

22 After ½ mile follow road round to **L**, cross bridge over river then at T-j at end of Stone Lane at top of short climb turn **R**.

23 Go through Axford following signs for Ramsbury. Climb through woodland.

← 3 pages

5 After ½ mile, as road swings left, bear **R** (in effect **SA**) 'Wolfhall, Crofton'.

6 Follow road round sharp left-hand and right-hand bends and past Crofton Beam Engines, ignoring turns to right and left.

7 At T-j on edge of Burbage turn **R** uphill (NS) then shortly at next T-j at end of Taskers Lane turn **R** (NS).

8 After ½ mile opposite Three Horseshoes PH bear **R** 'Durley, Savernake' onto Stibb Green then after further ½ mile turn first **L** by ornate brick house 'Easton Royal, Pewsey'.

9 At X-roads with A346 go **SA** 'Ram Alley'.

Along the Kennet valley & onto the downs north of Hungerford

The valley of the River Kennet has been a transport route since Roman times and is now shared by river, canal, railway and two parallel roads. The A4 uses the north side of the valley; to the south is a much more attractive alternative, slipping away quietly from Hungerford's broad High Street, crossing the tree-lined parkland of Hungerford Common and passing through the old red-brick village of Kintbury. Keep following the valley eastwards, crossing the canal and river near Marsh Benham, then turn north beyond Bagnor along a delightful quiet lane running parallel with a lovely clear stream, a tributary of the River Lambourn. You will run alongside an extraordinarily tall and long yew hedge north of Bagnor. Climb to the ride's first highpoint in the village of Chaddleworth (570ft / 174m) before a fast descent along the busier A338 to Great Shefford to rejoin the Lambourn Valley ('Valley of the Racehorse'). A short steep climb south from East Garston leads to the highpoint of the ride. After crossing the M4 it is mainly downhill (with one small dip) all the way back to Hungerford and a wide choice of refreshments.

Overview

On-road ● **31 miles / 50 kilometres** ● **Easy / Moderate**

Start
The clocktower in Hungerford

Parking
On Church Street, off the High Street near the clocktower

Busy roads
● About 1 mile on the A338 north of Great Shefford **20** to **21**

● Short section on A4 and A338 back into Hungerford (30mph speed limit) **25** to **26**

Terrain
Undulating with two noticeable climbs out of the Lambourn Valley

Nearest railway
Hungerford

Refreshments
Hungerford
Lots of choice

Kintbury
Lots of choice (3 pubs)

Marsh Benham
Red House PH
T: 01635 582017

Stockcross
Rising Sun PH
T: 01488 608131

Speen
Five Bells PH
T: 01635 48763

Bagnor
Blackbird PH
T: 01635 40638

Winterbourne
Winterbourne Arms PH
T: 01635 248200

Chieveley
Red Lion PH
T: 01635 248379

Leckhampstead
Stag PH
T: 01488 638436

Chaddleworth
Ibex Inn
T: 01488 638311

Great Shefford
Swan PH
T: 01488 648271

Other rides nearby

Ride 9
Page 56

Map pages

Other rides nearby

Ride 9
Page 56

Ride 10

Ride 12
Page 74

Ride 11
Page 68

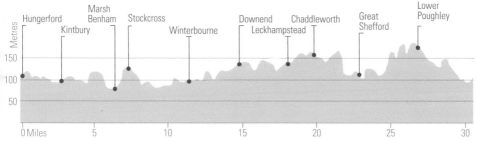

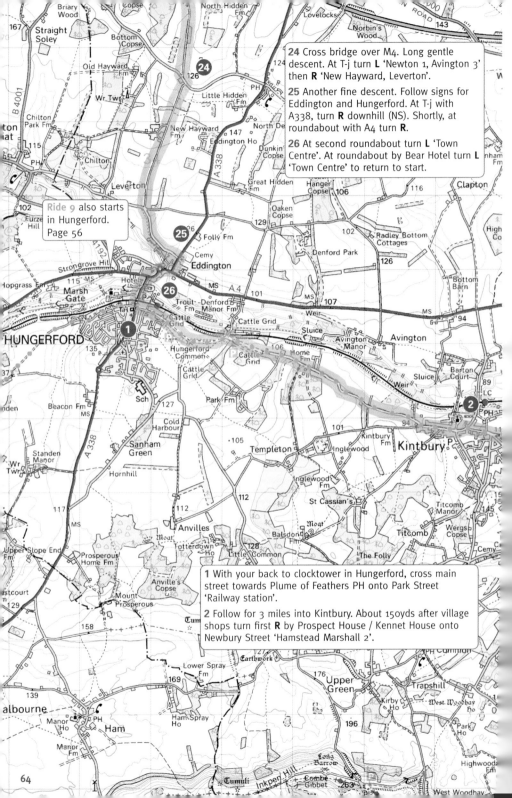

24 Cross bridge over M4. Long gentle descent. At T-j turn **L** 'Newton 1, Avington 3' then **R** 'New Hayward, Leverton'.

25 Another fine descent. Follow signs for Eddington and Hungerford. At T-j with A338, turn **R** downhill (NS). Shortly, at roundabout with A4 turn **R**.

26 At second roundabout turn **L** 'Town Centre'. At roundabout by Bear Hotel turn **L** 'Town Centre' to return to start.

Ride 9 also starts in Hungerford. Page 56

1 With your back to clocktower in Hungerford, cross main street towards Plume of Feathers PH onto Park Street 'Railway station'.

2 Follow for 3 miles into Kintbury. About 150yds after village shops turn first **R** by Prospect House / Kennet House onto Newbury Street 'Hamstead Marshall 2'.

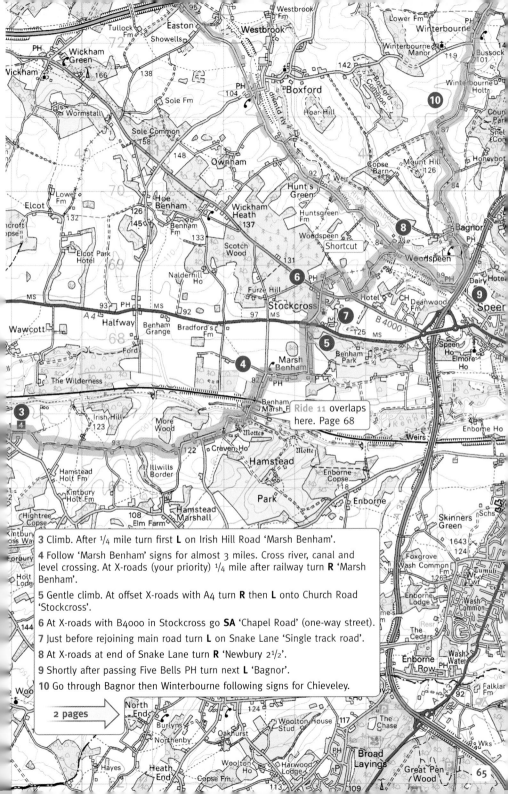

3 Climb. After ¼ mile turn first **L** on Irish Hill Road 'Marsh Benham'.

4 Follow 'Marsh Benham' signs for almost 3 miles. Cross river, canal and level crossing. At X-roads (your priority) ¼ mile after railway turn **R** 'Marsh Benham'.

5 Gentle climb. At offset X-roads with A4 turn **R** then **L** onto Church Road 'Stockcross'.

6 At X-roads with B4000 in Stockcross go **SA** 'Chapel Road' (one-way street).

7 Just before rejoining main road turn **L** on Snake Lane 'Single track road'.

8 At X-roads at end of Snake Lane turn **R** 'Newbury 2½'.

9 Shortly after passing Five Bells PH turn next **L** 'Bagnor'.

10 Go through Bagnor then Winterbourne following signs for Chieveley.

Ride **11** overlaps here. Page 68

2 pages →

65

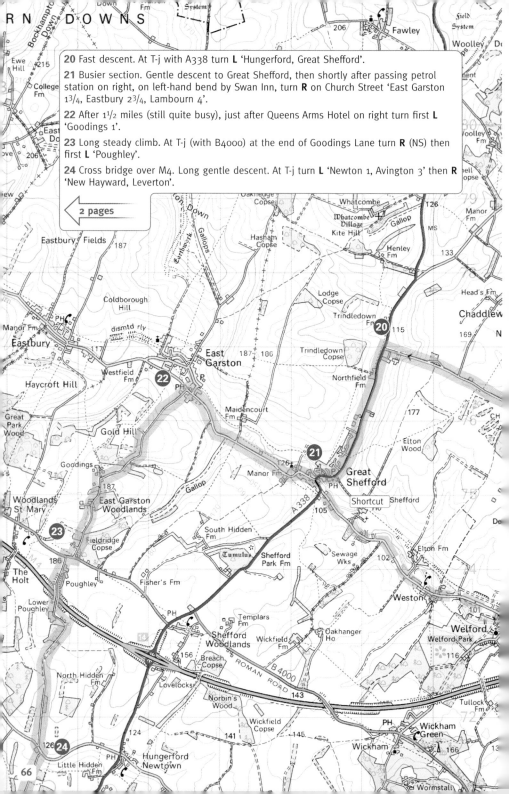

20 Fast descent. At T-j with A338 turn **L** 'Hungerford, Great Shefford'.

21 Busier section. Gentle descent to Great Shefford, then shortly after passing petrol station on right, on left-hand bend by Swan Inn, turn **R** on Church Street 'East Garston 1¾, Eastbury 2¾, Lambourn 4'.

22 After 1½ miles (still quite busy), just after Queens Arms Hotel on right turn first **L** 'Goodings 1'.

23 Long steady climb. At T-j (with B4000) at the end of Goodings Lane turn **R** (NS) then first **L** 'Poughley'.

24 Cross bridge over M4. Long gentle descent. At T-j turn **L** 'Newton 1, Avington 3' then **R** 'New Hayward, Leverton'.

2 pages

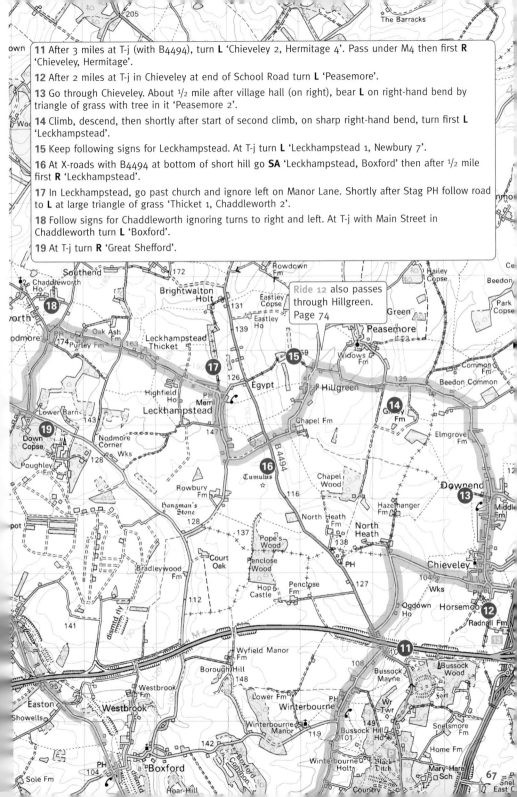

11 After 3 miles at T-j (with B4494), turn **L** 'Chieveley 2, Hermitage 4'. Pass under M4 then first **R** 'Chieveley, Hermitage'.

12 After 2 miles at T-j in Chieveley at end of School Road turn **L** 'Peasemore'.

13 Go through Chieveley. About ½ mile after village hall (on right), bear **L** on right-hand bend by triangle of grass with tree in it 'Peasemore 2'.

14 Climb, descend, then shortly after start of second climb, on sharp right-hand bend, turn first **L** 'Leckhampstead'.

15 Keep following signs for Leckhampstead. At T-j turn **L** 'Leckhampstead 1, Newbury 7'.

16 At X-roads with B4494 at bottom of short hill go **SA** 'Leckhampstead, Boxford' then after ½ mile first **R** 'Leckhampstead'.

17 In Leckhampstead, go past church and ignore left on Manor Lane. Shortly after Stag PH follow road to **L** at large triangle of grass 'Thicket 1, Chaddleworth 2'.

18 Follow signs for Chaddleworth ignoring turns to right and left. At T-j with Main Street in Chaddleworth turn **L** 'Boxford'.

19 At T-j turn **R** 'Great Shefford'.

Ride **12** also passes through Hillgreen. Page 74

Kingsclere, Newbury & the Kennet & Avon Canal

his is the only road
ride in the book which
is not appropriate for
lightweight road bikes with
narrow tyres: a long section
of the Kennet & Avon Canal
towpath is used from near
Thatcham to Hamstead
Park and there are short
stretches with roots across
the path. Having said this,
fitting 28mm tyres should
be sufficient as we are not
talking about mountain bike
territory. The ride wiggles its
way north parallel with the
A339 towards Thatcham then
sneaks across the corner of
the old Greenham Common
airbase on a new cyclepath
that links to a good stone
bridleway to drop you right
down on the Kennet & Avon
Canal towpath. The 7 miles

alongside the canal should
be taken at a leisurely pace
as there are often walkers on
the towpath, especially in the
centre of Newbury. For much
of the canal section the ride
is following the course of
National Cycle Network Route
4 which runs all the way from

St David's in Pembrokeshire
to the centre of London.
Soon after leaving the canal
near to Hamstead Park the
ride turns south to explore
the bewildering network of
lanes nestling below the
steep chalk escarpment of
the North Hampshire Downs,
which rise to a highpoint of
975ft (297m) on Walbury
Hill. Follow the instructions
carefully as you thread your
way south then east through
woodland, crossing the A343
and A34 to the north of
Highclere Castle. Pass beneath
the slopes of Watership Down
(of rabbit fame) and over
the rise of the oddly named
Nothing Hill before dropping
back down to the start in
Kingsclere.

Overview

On-road ● **29 miles / 47 kilometres** ● **Moderate**

Start
Kingsclere (or Newbury)

Parking
Car park near church
in Kingsclere

Busy roads
None

Terrain
Flat along the canal,
undulating before and after

Nearest railway
Thatcham or Newbury

Refreshments
Kingsclere
Lots of choice

Newbury
Lots of choice

Ball Hill
Furze Bush Inn
T: 01635 253228

Burghclere
Carpenters Arms
T: 01635 278251

Ecchinswell
Royal Oak PH
T: 01635 291337

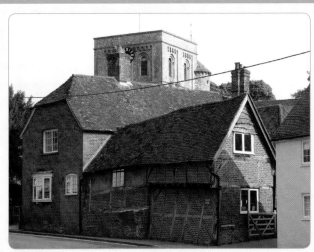

Other rides nearby

Ride 10
Page 62

Ride 11

Map pages

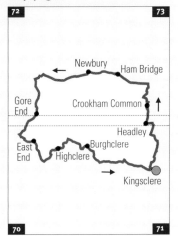

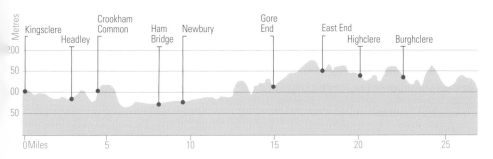

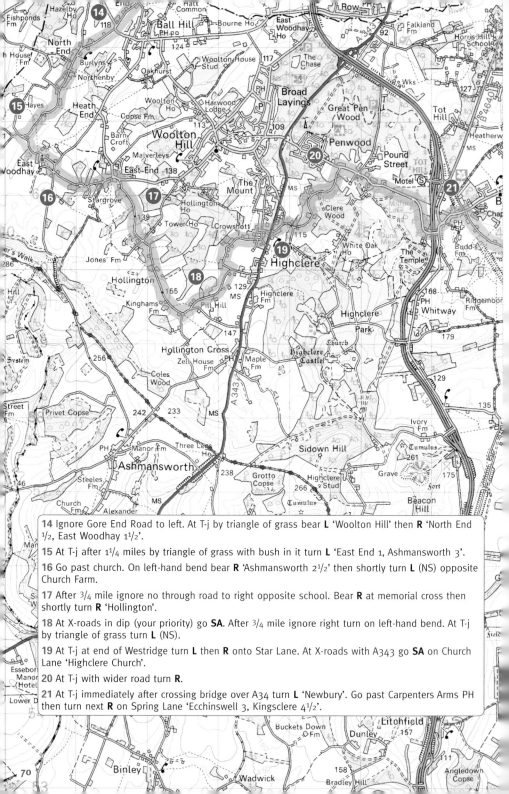

14 Ignore Gore End Road to left. At T-j by triangle of grass bear **L** 'Woolton Hill' then **R** 'North End' ¹/₂, East Woodhay 1¹/₂'.

15 At T-j after 1¹/₄ miles by triangle of grass with bush in it turn **L** 'East End 1, Ashmansworth 3'.

16 Go past church. On left-hand bend bear **R** 'Ashmansworth 2¹/₂' then shortly turn **L** (NS) opposite Church Farm.

17 After ³/₄ mile ignore no through road to right opposite school. Bear **R** at memorial cross then shortly turn **R** 'Hollington'.

18 At X-roads in dip (your priority) go **SA**. After ³/₄ mile ignore right turn on left-hand bend. At T-j by triangle of grass turn **L** (NS).

19 At T-j at end of Westridge turn **L** then **R** onto Star Lane. At X-roads with A343 go **SA** on Church Lane 'Highclere Church'.

20 At T-j with wider road turn **R**.

21 At T-j immediately after crossing bridge over A34 turn **L** 'Newbury'. Go past Carpenters Arms PH then turn next **R** on Spring Lane 'Ecchinswell 3, Kingsclere 4¹/₂'.

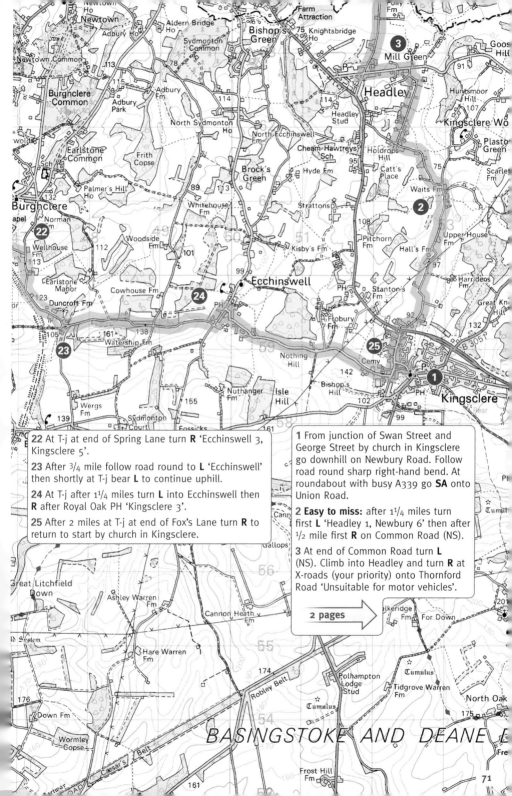

22 At T-j at end of Spring Lane turn **R** 'Ecchinswell 3, Kingsclere 5'.

23 After 3/4 mile follow road round to **L** 'Ecchinswell' then shortly at T-j bear **L** to continue uphill.

24 At T-j after 1¼ miles turn **L** into Ecchinswell then **R** after Royal Oak PH 'Kingsclere 3'.

25 After 2 miles at T-j at end of Fox's Lane turn **R** to return to start by church in Kingsclere.

1 From junction of Swan Street and George Street by church in Kingsclere go downhill on Newbury Road. Follow road round sharp right-hand bend. At roundabout with busy A339 go **SA** onto Union Road.

2 Easy to miss: after 1¼ miles turn first **L** 'Headley 1, Newbury 6' then after ½ mile first **R** on Common Road (NS).

3 At end of Common Road turn **L** (NS). Climb into Headley and turn **R** at X-roads (your priority) onto Thornford Road 'Unsuitable for motor vehicles'.

2 pages ➡

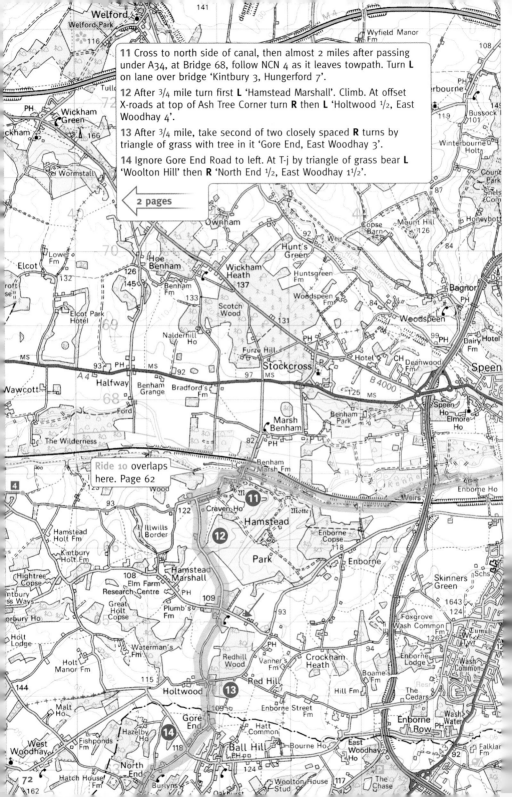

11 Cross to north side of canal, then almost 2 miles after passing under A34, at Bridge 68, follow NCN 4 as it leaves towpath. Turn **L** on lane over bridge 'Kintbury 3, Hungerford 7'.

12 After ¾ mile turn first **L** 'Hamstead Marshall'. Climb. At offset X-roads at top of Ash Tree Corner turn **R** then **L** 'Holtwood ½, East Woodhay 4'.

13 After ¾ mile, take second of two closely spaced **R** turns by triangle of grass with tree in it 'Gore End, East Woodhay 3'.

14 Ignore Gore End Road to left. At T-j by triangle of grass bear **L** 'Woolton Hill' then **R** 'North End ½, East Woodhay 1½'.

2 pages

Ride 10 overlaps here. Page 62

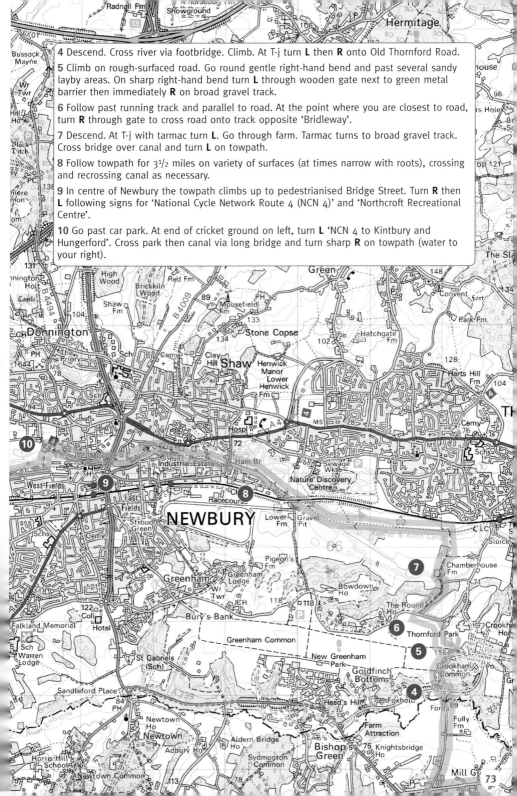

4 Descend. Cross river via footbridge. Climb. At T-j turn **L** then **R** onto Old Thornford Road.

5 Climb on rough-surfaced road. Go round gentle right-hand bend and past several sandy layby areas. On sharp right-hand bend turn **L** through wooden gate next to green metal barrier then immediately **R** on broad gravel track.

6 Follow past running track and parallel to road. At the point where you are closest to road, turn **R** through gate to cross road onto track opposite 'Bridleway'.

7 Descend. At T-j with tarmac turn **L**. Go through farm. Tarmac turns to broad gravel track. Cross bridge over canal and turn **L** on towpath.

8 Follow towpath for 3½ miles on variety of surfaces (at times narrow with roots), crossing and recrossing canal as necessary.

9 In centre of Newbury the towpath climbs up to pedestrianised Bridge Street. Turn **R** then **L** following signs for 'National Cycle Network Route 4 (NCN 4)' and 'Northcroft Recreational Centre'.

10 Go past car park. At end of cricket ground on left, turn **L** 'NCN 4 to Kintbury and Hungerford'. Cross park then canal via long bridge and turn sharp **R** on towpath (water to your right).

73

Chalk downland between East Ilsley, Boxford & Frilsham

South of Oxford the land rises to over 600ft (180m) on the chalk downs crossed by the ancient trackway known as the Ridgeway. East Ilsley is a small village just to the south of the Ridgeway. The ride climbs to Stanmore passing the vast undulating fields that characterise this part of the world, a real contrast to the thickly wooded hills of the Chilterns, just a few miles to the east, on the other side of the Thames valley. The village of Beedon is full of big old sumptuous

red-brick houses and barns, a throwback to the time this was on the main road from Newbury to Oxford. Drop down through Hampstead Norreys into the valley formed by the infant River Pang (as in Pangbourne) before a steeper climb towards Aldworth and the distinctive pub sign at the Four Points Inn. Descend then climb again as you turn west towards the sandy pine woodlands around Hermitage, representing a contrast to the chalk landscape that dominates to the north, south and west. The route west

from Frilsham threads its way, seemingly against the odds, on a series of quiet lanes through Wellhouse, Longlane, Curridge and Winterbourne, managing to avoid the busy roads radiating out of Newbury, a few miles to the south. Once you reach Boxford, set in the Lambourn valley, you are back in the land of big open grasslands on the rolling chalk. A long gentle climb through Peasemore brings you to the outward route at Stanmore, setting you up for a fine fast descent to end the ride.

Overview

On-road ● **34 miles / 54 kilometres** ● **Moderate**

Start
East Ilsley, just off the A34
southwest of Didcot

Parking
On street

Busy roads
None

Terrain
Undulating. Two noticeable
climbs: at the start from East
Ilsley to Stanmore and
between Hampstead Norreys
and Aldworth

Nearest railway
Didcot

Refreshments

East Ilsley
Crown & Horns PH
T: 01635 281545
Swan PH
T: 01635 281238

World's End (Beedon)
Coach PH
T:01635 247271

Aldworth
Four Points PH
T: 01635 578367

Yattendon
Royal Oak PH
T: 01635 201325

Curridge
Bunk Inn
T: 01635 200400

Winterbourne
Winterbourne Arms PH
T: 01635 248200

Peasemore
Fox & Hounds PH
T: 01635 248252

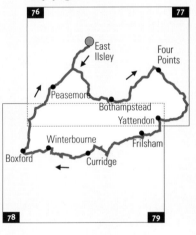

Map pages

Other rides nearby

Ride 10
Page 62

Ride 12

Ride 13
Page 80

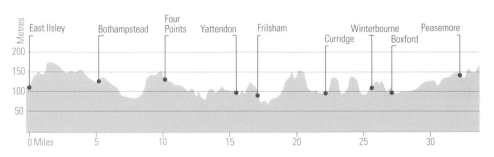

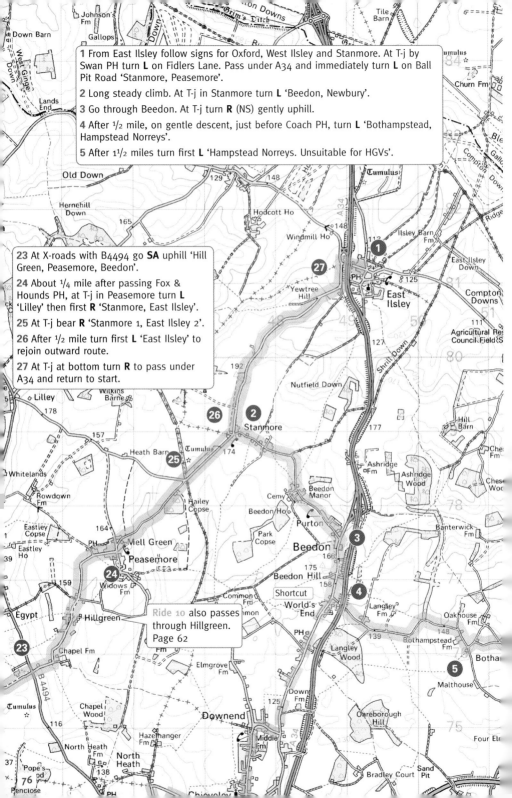

1 From East Ilsley follow signs for Oxford, West Ilsley and Stanmore. At T-j by Swan PH turn **L** on Fidlers Lane. Pass under A34 and immediately turn **L** on Ball Pit Road 'Stanmore, Peasemore'.

2 Long steady climb. At T-j in Stanmore turn **L** 'Beedon, Newbury'.

3 Go through Beedon. At T-j turn **R** (NS) gently uphill.

4 After ½ mile, on gentle descent, just before Coach PH, turn **L** 'Bothampstead, Hampstead Norreys'.

5 After 1½ miles turn first **L** 'Hampstead Norreys. Unsuitable for HGVs'.

23 At X-roads with B4494 go **SA** uphill 'Hill Green, Peasemore, Beedon'.

24 About ¼ mile after passing Fox & Hounds PH, at T-j in Peasemore turn **L** 'Lilley' then first **R** 'Stanmore, East Ilsley'.

25 At T-j bear **R** 'Stanmore 1, East Ilsley 2'.

26 After ½ mile turn first **L** 'East Ilsley' to rejoin outward route.

27 At T-j at bottom turn **R** to pass under A34 and return to start.

Ride 10 also passes through Hillgreen. Page 62

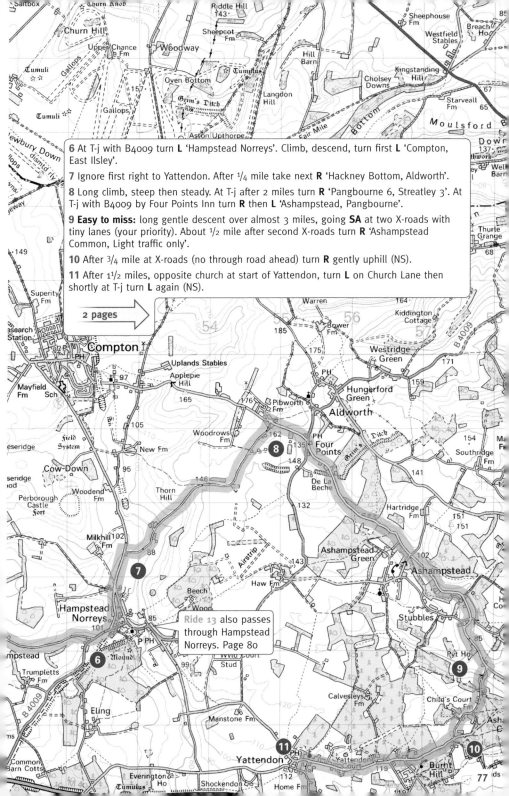

6 At T-j with B4009 turn **L** 'Hampstead Norreys'. Climb, descend, turn first **L** 'Compton, East Ilsley'.

7 Ignore first right to Yattendon. After ¼ mile take next **R** 'Hackney Bottom, Aldworth'.

8 Long climb, steep then steady. At T-j after 2 miles turn **R** 'Pangbourne 6, Streatley 3'. At T-j with B4009 by Four Points Inn turn **R** then **L** 'Ashampstead, Pangbourne'.

9 Easy to miss: long gentle descent over almost 3 miles, going **SA** at two X-roads with tiny lanes (your priority). About ½ mile after second X-roads turn **R** 'Ashampstead Common, Light traffic only'.

10 After ¾ mile at X-roads (no through road ahead) turn **R** gently uphill (NS).

11 After 1½ miles, opposite church at start of Yattendon, turn **L** on Church Lane then shortly at T-j turn **L** again (NS).

2 pages

Ride 13 also passes through Hampstead Norreys. Page 80

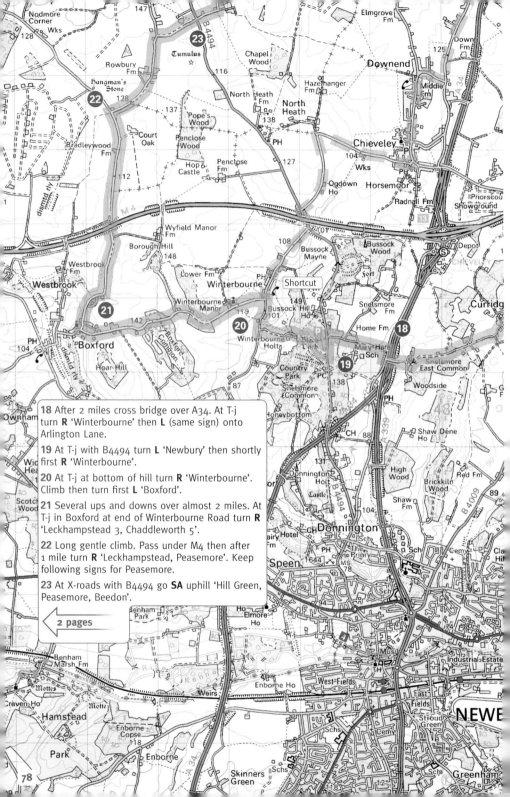

18 After 2 miles cross bridge over A34. At T-j turn **R** 'Winterbourne' then **L** (same sign) onto Arlington Lane.

19 At T-j with B4494 turn **L** 'Newbury' then shortly first **R** 'Winterbourne'.

20 At T-j at bottom of hill turn **R** 'Winterbourne'. Climb then turn first **L** 'Boxford'.

21 Several ups and downs over almost 2 miles. At T-j in Boxford at end of Winterbourne Road turn **R** 'Leckhampstead 3, Chaddleworth 5'.

22 Long gentle climb. Pass under M4 then after 1 mile turn **R** 'Leckhampstead, Peasemore'. Keep following signs for Peasemore.

23 At X-roads with B4494 go **SA** uphill 'Hill Green, Peasemore, Beedon'.

◁ **2 pages**

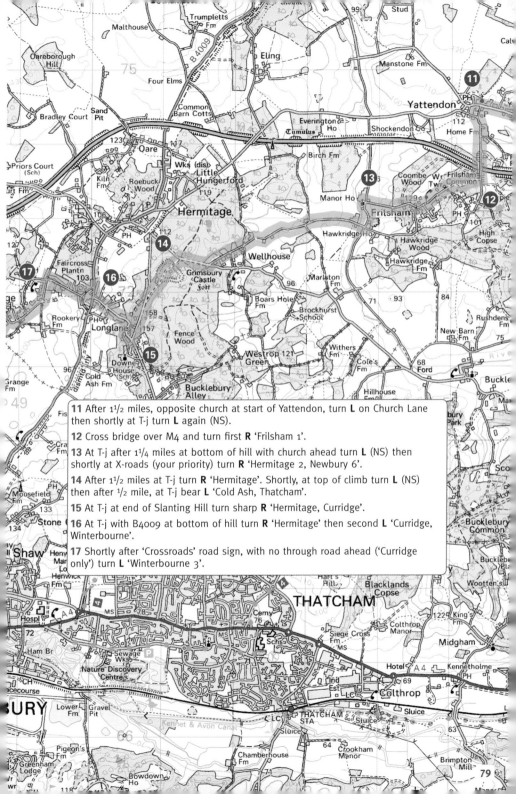

11 After 1¹/₂ miles, opposite church at start of Yattendon, turn **L** on Church Lane then shortly at T-j turn **L** again (NS).

12 Cross bridge over M4 and turn first **R** 'Frilsham 1'.

13 At T-j after 1¹/₄ miles at bottom of hill with church ahead turn **L** (NS) then shortly at X-roads (your priority) turn **R** 'Hermitage 2, Newbury 6'.

14 After 1¹/₂ miles at T-j turn **R** 'Hermitage'. Shortly, at top of climb turn **L** (NS) then after ¹/₂ mile, at T-j bear **L** 'Cold Ash, Thatcham'.

15 At T-j at end of Slanting Hill turn sharp **R** 'Hermitage, Curridge'.

16 At T-j with B4009 at bottom of hill turn **R** 'Hermitage' then second **L** 'Curridge, Winterbourne'.

17 Shortly after 'Crossroads' road sign, with no through road ahead ('Curridge only') turn **L** 'Winterbourne 3'.

From Goring to Pangbourne along the Pang valley & onto the downs

The Goring Gap is the name given to the valley formed by the River Thames as it cuts through the long ridge of chalk upland stretching from the Salisbury Plain in the west to Newmarket and beyond in the east. This ride explores both sides of the river and starts by climbing east from Goring through lovely beechwoods up to Woodcote. Turning south then west and dropping back down into the Thames valley you pass the unusual sight of hundreds of alpacas grazing peacefully in the fields surrounding Bozedown Farm, just east of Whitchurch. A short busy section takes you south of the Thames via the Toll Bridge at Pangbourne (home of Kenneth Grahame, author of *Wind in the Willows*) then back onto the network of quiet lanes leading southwest past Bradfield and Stanford Dingley along the valley of the River Pang. This becomes a clear, fast-flowing stream running alongside lines of tall poplars as you turn north past Frilsham Church to pass under the M4 and climb through Hampstead Norreys and up towards Aldworth. The ride finishes with a fast whoosh down the B4009 to the bridge over the Thames and a return to the delights of Goring.

Overview

On-road ● 26 miles / 42 kilometres ● Moderate

Start
Ye Miller of Mansfield PH, High Street, Goring

Parking
Follow Manor Road opposite Ye Miller of Mansfield

Busy roads
● Short busy section on B471 and A329 through Pangbourne **8**

● B4009 Aldworth to Goring, although half of this is downhill **19**

Terrain
Three noticeable climbs, the longest (450ft / 135m) at the start from Goring to the highest point of the ride at Woodcote. The others are southwest of Pangbourne then northeast from Hampstead Norreys towards Aldworth

Other rides nearby

Ride 12
Page 74

Ride 13

Ride 14
Page 86

Nearest railway
Pangbourne or Goring

Refreshments
Goring & Pangbourne
Lots of choice

Stanford Dingley (just off route)
Bull PH
T: 0118 974 4582
Old Boot PH
T: 0118 974 4292

Hampstead Norreys
White Hart PH
T: 01635 202248

Aldworth
Four Points PH
T: 01635 578367
Bell PH
T: 01635 578272

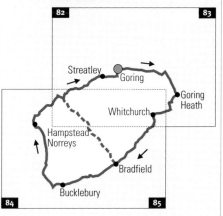

Map pages

82   83

Streatley   Goring

Goring Heath

Whitchurch

Hampstead Norreys

Bradfield

Bucklebury

84   85

Goring   Goring   Whitchurch   Bradfield   Streatley
                Heath   Bucklebury   Hampstead
                                                                 Norreys

Metres
200
150
100
50

0 Miles   5   10   15   20   25

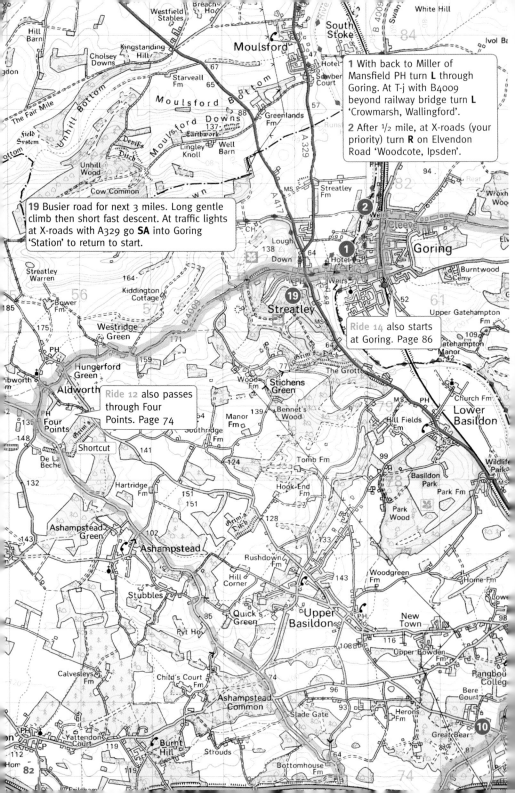

1 With back to Miller of Mansfield PH turn **L** through Goring. At T-j with B4009 beyond railway bridge turn **L** 'Crowmarsh, Wallingford'.

2 After ½ mile, at X-roads (your priority) turn **R** on Elvendon Road 'Woodcote, Ipsden'.

19 Busier road for next 3 miles. Long gentle climb then short fast descent. At traffic lights at X-roads with A329 go **SA** into Goring 'Station' to return to start.

Ride **14** also starts at Goring. Page 86

Ride **12** also passes through Four Points. Page 74

Shortcut

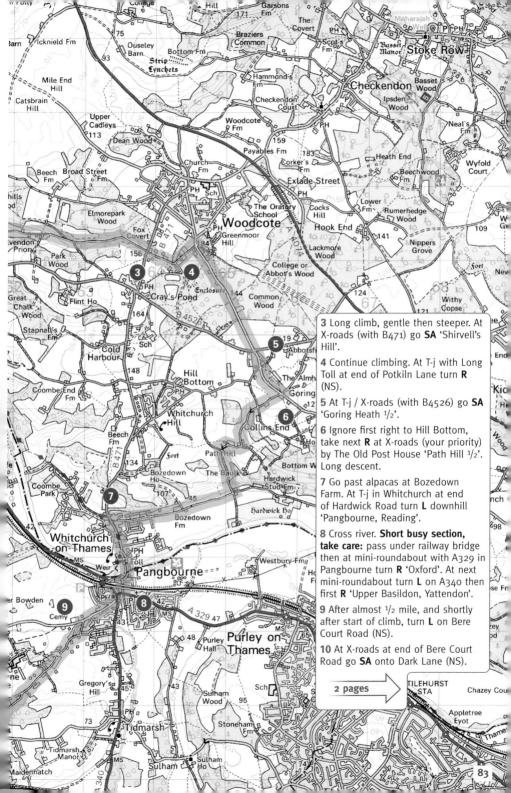

3 Long climb, gentle then steeper. At X-roads (with B471) go **SA** 'Shirvell's Hill'.

4 Continue climbing. At T-j with Long Toll at end of Potkiln Lane turn **R** (NS).

5 At T-j / X-roads (with B4526) go **SA** 'Goring Heath 1/2'.

6 Ignore first right to Hill Bottom, take next **R** at X-roads (your priority) by The Old Post House 'Path Hill 1/2'. Long descent.

7 Go past alpacas at Bozedown Farm. At T-j in Whitchurch at end of Hardwick Road turn **L** downhill 'Pangbourne, Reading'.

8 Cross river. **Short busy section, take care:** pass under railway bridge then at mini-roundabout with A329 in Pangbourne turn **R** 'Oxford'. At next mini-roundabout turn **L** on A340 then first **R** 'Upper Basildon, Yattendon'.

9 After almost 1/2 mile, and shortly after start of climb, turn **L** on Bere Court Road (NS).

10 At X-roads at end of Bere Court Road go **SA** onto Dark Lane (NS).

2 pages →

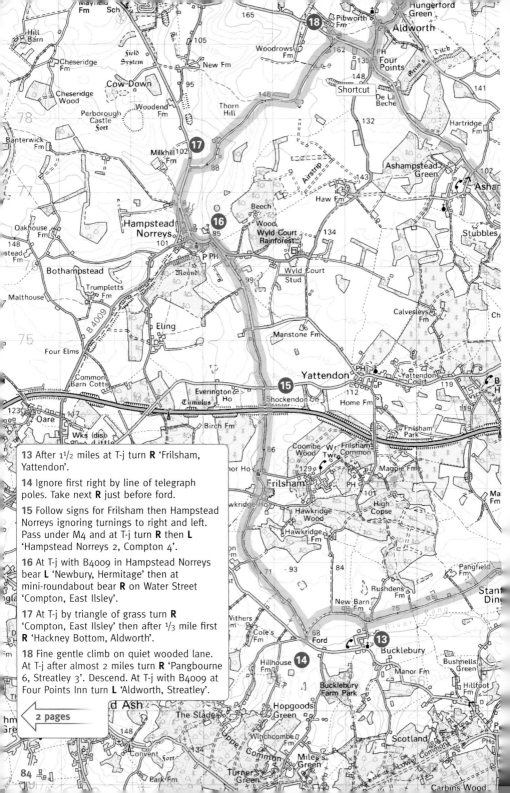

13 After 1¹/₂ miles at T-j turn **R** 'Frilsham, Yattendon'.

14 Ignore first right by line of telegraph poles. Take next **R** just before ford.

15 Follow signs for Frilsham then Hampstead Norreys ignoring turnings to right and left. Pass under M4 and at T-j turn **R** then **L** 'Hampstead Norreys 2, Compton 4'.

16 At T-j with B4009 in Hampstead Norreys bear **L** 'Newbury, Hermitage' then at mini-roundabout bear **R** on Water Street 'Compton, East Ilsley'.

17 At T-j by triangle of grass turn **R** 'Compton, East Ilsley' then after ¹/₃ mile first **R** 'Hackney Bottom, Aldworth'.

18 Fine gentle climb on quiet wooded lane. At T-j after almost 2 miles turn **R** 'Pangbourne 6, Streatley 3'. Descend. At T-j with B4009 at Four Points Inn turn **L** 'Aldworth, Streatley'.

◀ 2 pages

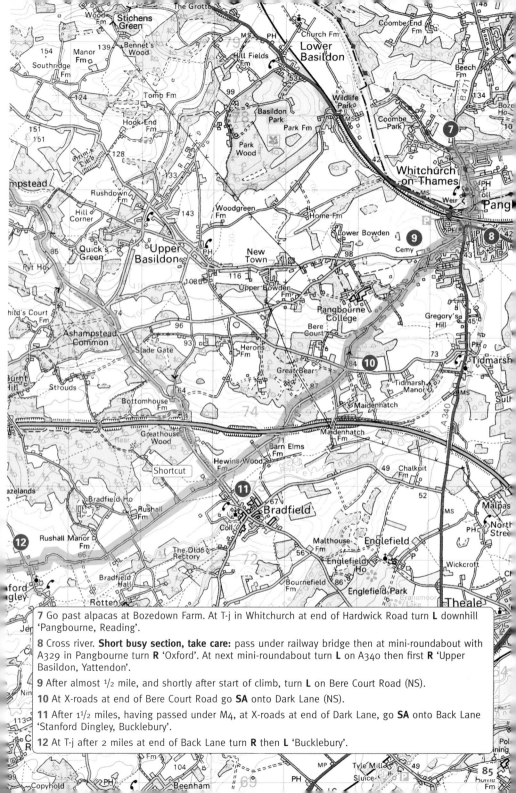

7 Go past alpacas at Bozedown Farm. At T-j in Whitchurch at end of Hardwick Road turn **L** downhill 'Pangbourne, Reading'.

8 Cross river. **Short busy section, take care:** pass under railway bridge then at mini-roundabout with A329 in Pangbourne turn **R** 'Oxford'. At next mini-roundabout turn **L** on A340 then first **R** 'Upper Basildon, Yattendon'.

9 After almost 1/2 mile, and shortly after start of climb, turn **L** on Bere Court Road (NS).

10 At X-roads at end of Bere Court Road go **SA** onto Dark Lane (NS).

11 After 1 1/2 miles, having passed under M4, at X-roads at end of Dark Lane, go **SA** onto Back Lane 'Stanford Dingley, Bucklebury'.

12 At T-j after 2 miles at end of Back Lane turn **R** then **L** 'Bucklebury'.

Through the Chilterns from Goring to Christmas Common

The chalk slopes of the Chilterns are covered with beechwoods and lush pastures. Since the 1960s some 300 square miles of the Chilterns have been designated an Area of Outstanding Natural Beauty. In the 19th century the area was a great centre for English furniture making and this resulted in continual tree planting. Today there are some 30,000 acres of beech woodlands. They provide a stunning background to cycle rides throughout the year but especially so in spring with carpets of bluebells, and in the autumn with the changing of colours. The ride heads north from Goring through an open landscape more akin to the rolling downland on the west side of the river. The climb is inevitable as you turn east up the wooded escarpment to Cookley Green and Christmas Common, the highest point of the ride. A plateau woodland section through Northend and Turville Heath is followed by a fast downhill to Middle Assendon. This being the Chilterns, what goes down must go up: another climb, this time short and steep takes you up to Bix and through to Stoke Row, famous for the Maharajah's Well, built in 1864. The well was sunk as a result of the friendship between the Maharajah of Benares and Mr Edward Anderdon Reade of Ipsden who became Governor of the Northwest Provinces. The Indian-style cupola was designed by Mr Reade and stands over the 364ft (111m) deep well. It was dug by two men in one year – a tremendous feat of Victorian skill. The ride finishes with a wonderful long wooded descent from Woodcote back down to the Thames at Goring.

Overview

On-road ● **32 miles / 52 kilometres** ● **Moderate / Strenuous**

Start
Ye Miller of Mansfield PH, High Street, Goring

Parking
Follow Manor Road opposite Ye Miller of Mansfield

Busy roads
Two short sections on the B481:

● Near Cookley Green ⑨ to ⑩

● To the east of Stoke Row ⑱

Terrain
The first half of the ride is almost all a climb (to the highpoint at Christmas Common). Two other climbs: Middle Assendon to Bix and Greys Green to Stoke Row

Nearest railway
Goring

Other rides nearby

Ride 14

Ride 13
Page 80

Ride 15
Page 92

Refreshments

Goring
Lots of choice

Christmas Common
Fox & Hounds PH
T: 01491 612599

Lower Assendon
Golden Ball PH
T: 01491 574157
Rainbow PH
T: 01491 574879

Stoke Row
Cherry Tree Inn
T: 01491 680430
Crooked Billet
T: 01491 681048

Checkendon
Black Horse PH
T: 01491 680418
Four Horseshoes PH
T: 01491 680325

Map pages

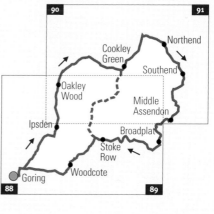

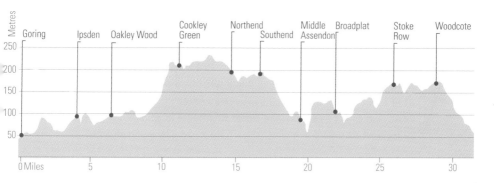

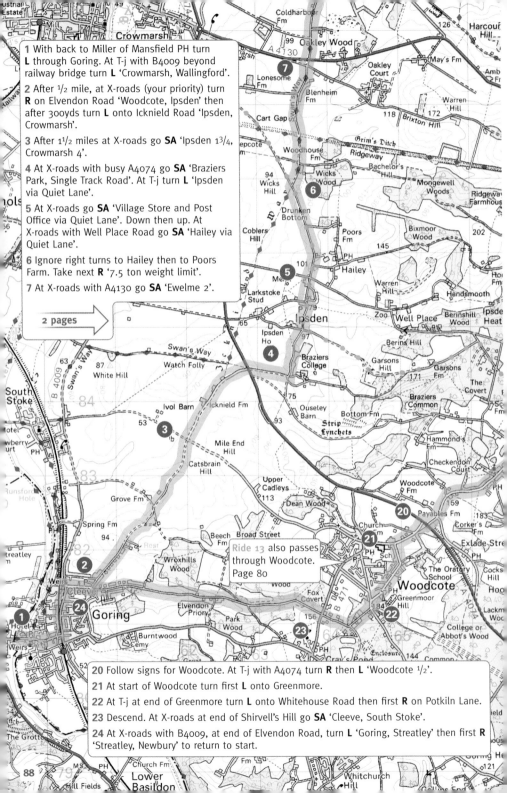

1 With back to Miller of Mansfield PH turn **L** through Goring. At T-j with B4009 beyond railway bridge turn **L** 'Crowmarsh, Wallingford'.

2 After ½ mile, at X-roads (your priority) turn **R** on Elvendon Road 'Woodcote, Ipsden' then after 300yds turn **L** onto Icknield Road 'Ipsden, Crowmarsh'.

3 After 1½ miles at X-roads go **SA** 'Ipsden 1¾, Crowmarsh 4'.

4 At X-roads with busy A4074 go **SA** 'Braziers Park, Single Track Road'. At T-j turn **L** 'Ipsden via Quiet Lane'.

5 At X-roads go **SA** 'Village Store and Post Office via Quiet Lane'. Down then up. At X-roads with Well Place Road go **SA** 'Hailey via Quiet Lane'.

6 Ignore right turns to Hailey then to Poors Farm. Take next **R** '7.5 ton weight limit'.

7 At X-roads with A4130 go **SA** 'Ewelme 2'.

2 pages ➡

Ride 13 also passes through Woodcote. Page 80

20 Follow signs for Woodcote. At T-j with A4074 turn **R** then **L** 'Woodcote ½'.

21 At start of Woodcote turn first **L** onto Greenmore.

22 At T-j at end of Greenmore turn **L** onto Whitehouse Road then first **R** on Potkiln Lane.

23 Descend. At X-roads at end of Shirvell's Hill go **SA** 'Cleeve, South Stoke'.

24 At X-roads with B4009, at end of Elvendon Road, turn **L** 'Goring, Streatley' then first **R** 'Streatley, Newbury' to return to start.

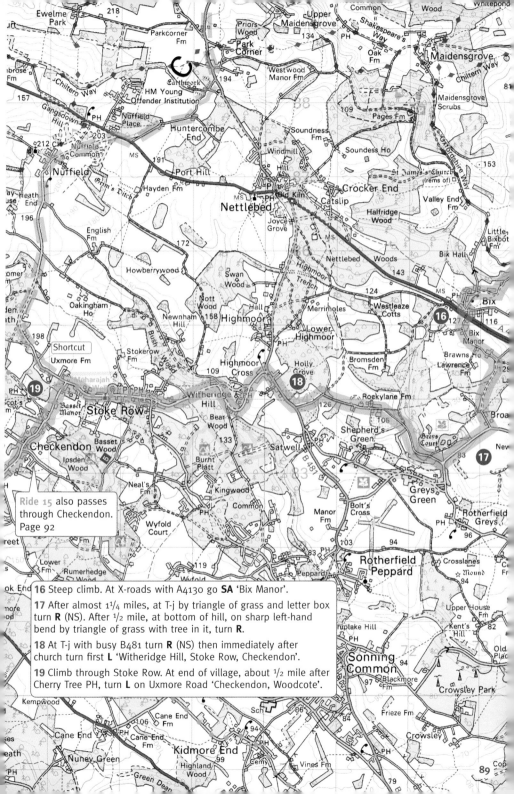

Ride 15 also passes through Checkendon. Page 92

16 Steep climb. At X-roads with A4130 go **SA** 'Bix Manor'.

17 After almost 1¼ miles, at T-j by triangle of grass and letter box turn **R** (NS). After ½ mile, at bottom of hill, on sharp left-hand bend by triangle of grass with tree in it, turn **R**.

18 At T-j with busy B481 turn **R** (NS) then immediately after church turn first **L** 'Witheridge Hill, Stoke Row, Checkendon'.

19 Climb through Stoke Row. At end of village, about ½ mile after Cherry Tree PH, turn **L** on Uxmore Road 'Checkendon, Woodcote'.

5 At X-roads go **SA** 'Village Store and Post Office via Quiet Lane'. Down then up. At X-roads with Well Place Road go **SA** 'Hailey via Quiet Lane'.

6 Ignore right turns to Hailey then to Poors Farm. Take next **R** '7.5 ton weight limit'.

7 At X-roads with A4130 go **SA** 'Ewelme 2'.

8 At T-j with wider road, on sharp bend turn **R** (NS). At offset X-roads with Old London Road turn **R** then **L** 'Swyncombe, Cookley Green'.

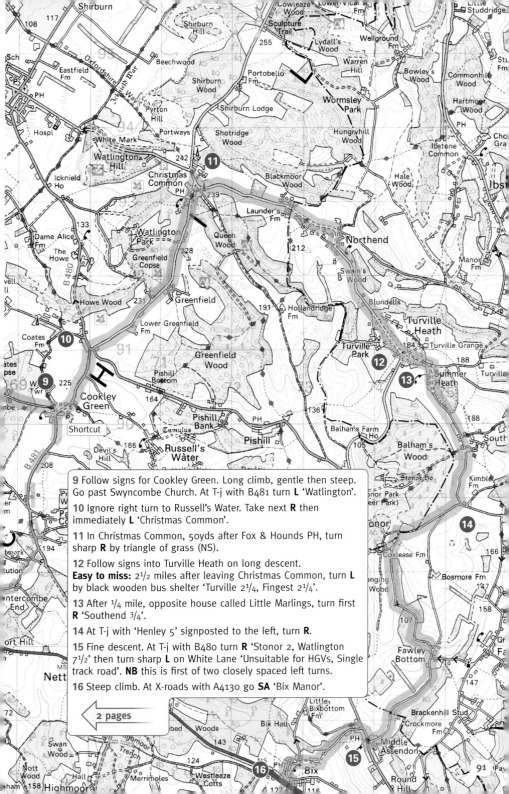

9 Follow signs for Cookley Green. Long climb, gentle then steep. Go past Swyncombe Church. At T-j with B481 turn **L** 'Watlington'.

10 Ignore right turn to Russell's Water. Take next **R** then immediately **L** 'Christmas Common'.

11 In Christmas Common, 50yds after Fox & Hounds PH, turn sharp **R** by triangle of grass (NS).

12 Follow signs into Turville Heath on long descent.
Easy to miss: 2½ miles after leaving Christmas Common, turn **L** by black wooden bus shelter 'Turville 2¼, Fingest 2¼'.

13 After ¼ mile, opposite house called Little Marlings, turn first **R** 'Southend ¾'.

14 At T-j with 'Henley 5' signposted to the left, turn **R**.

15 Fine descent. At T-j with B480 turn **R** 'Stonor 2, Watlington 7½' then turn sharp **L** on White Lane 'Unsuitable for HGVs, Single track road'. **NB** this is first of two closely spaced left turns.

16 Steep climb. At X-roads with A4130 go **SA** 'Bix Manor'.

2 pages

West of Henley through Chiltern beechwoods

T he Chiltern beechwoods are always a delight to cycle through, passing beneath a cathedral of smooth-limbed boughs and a canopy of green. The area is also well served by a range of excellent pubs. Henley's reputation is based on its annual regatta on the River Thames which flows right through the heart of the town. The first University Boat Race took place here in 1829 and within 10 years it was a national event enjoying royal patronage. The 18th-century bridge over the river is decorated with the faces of Father Thames and the goddess Isis. The first mile of the ride on the unavoidable A4155 is busy but the contrast

as soon as you turn off on the minor road to Fawley is extraordinary. Gone are the noise and traffic, replaced by a quiet lane climbing steadily for several miles through lovely woodland to the ride's first highpoint just

beyond Southend. After a fast descent to Stonor, a second climb follows, again beneath beech canopy, through the small clusters of houses at Maidensgrove and Russell's Water to the second highpoint at Cookley Green. After almost 2 miles of gentle descent on this slightly busier road you rejoin the lane network to Nuffield and Checkendon. The best descent of the day drops gently over several miles from Checkendon to the rather sinister-sounding Gallowstree Common. The trend is still downwards as you bypass Sonning Common and Binfield Heath to approach Henley from the south, past the golf course and through Harpsden.

Overview
On-road ● 29 miles / 47 kilometres ● Moderate / Strenuous

Start
The Market Place, Henley-on-Thames

Parking
Long-stay car park near the railway station

Busy roads
● The exit from Henley on the A4155 ❶ to ❸

● The B481 south from Cookley Green (gently downhill) ❽ to ❾

Terrain
Two main climbs, one from near the start up through Fawley to Southend (525ft / 160m) and a second from Stonor up to Cookley Green (445ft / 135m). The second half of the ride is less hilly

Nearest railway
Henley

Other rides nearby

Ride 14
Page 86

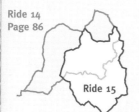

Ride 15

Refreshments

Henley
Lots of choice

Maidensgrove
Five Horseshoes PH
01491 641 282

Nuffield
Crown PH
T: 01491 641335

Sonning Common
Butchers Arms PH
T: 0118 972 3101

Binfield Heath
Bottle & Glass PH
T: 01491 575755

Map pages

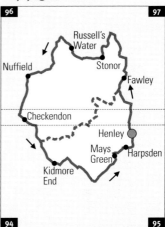

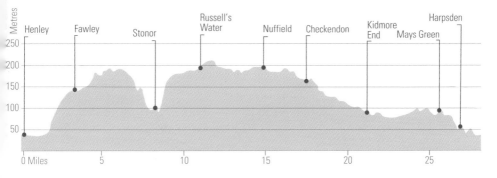

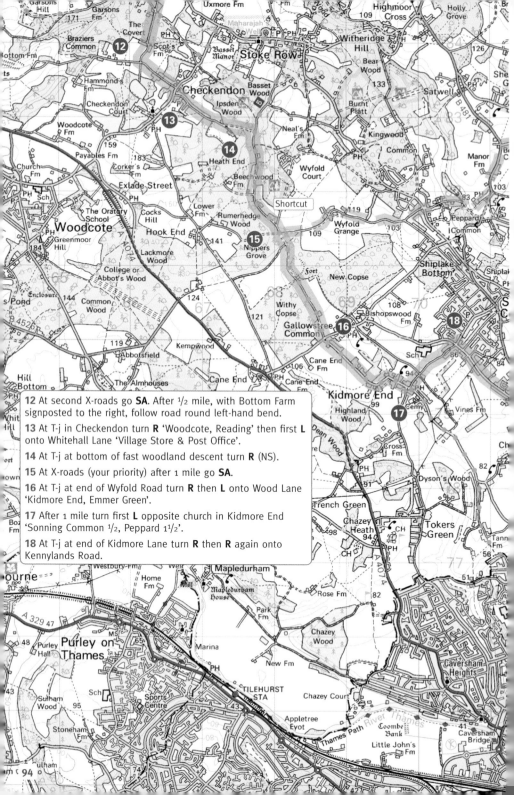

12 At second X-roads go **SA**. After ¹/₂ mile, with Bottom Farm signposted to the right, follow road round left-hand bend.

13 At T-j in Checkendon turn **R** 'Woodcote, Reading' then first **L** onto Whitehall Lane 'Village Store & Post Office'.

14 At T-j at bottom of fast woodland descent turn **R** (NS).

15 At X-roads (your priority) after 1 mile go **SA**.

16 At T-j at end of Wyfold Road turn **R** then **L** onto Wood Lane 'Kidmore End, Emmer Green'.

17 After 1 mile turn first **L** opposite church in Kidmore End 'Sonning Common ¹/₂, Peppard 1¹/₂'.

18 At T-j at end of Kidmore Lane turn **R** then **R** again onto Kennylands Road.

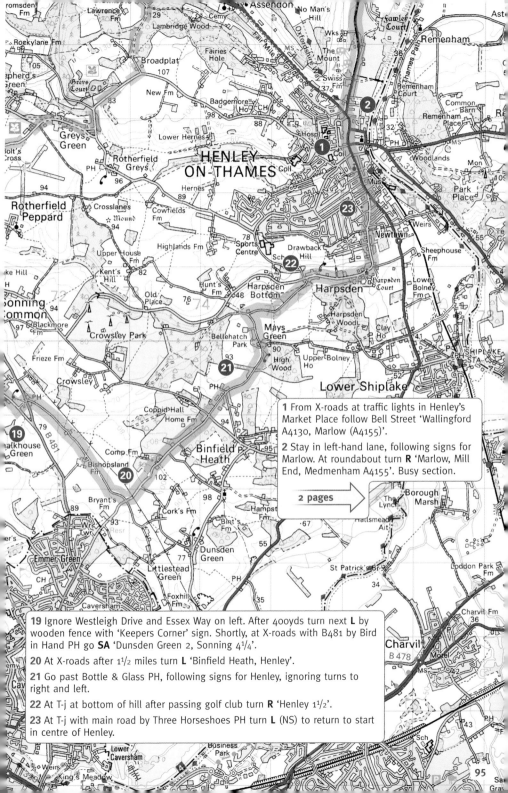

1 From X-roads at traffic lights in Henley's Market Place follow Bell Street 'Wallingford A4130, Marlow (A4155)'.

2 Stay in left-hand lane, following signs for Marlow. At roundabout turn **R** 'Marlow, Mill End, Medmenham A4155'. Busy section.

2 pages →

19 Ignore Westleigh Drive and Essex Way on left. After 400yds turn next **L** by wooden fence with 'Keepers Corner' sign. Shortly, at X-roads with B481 by Bird in Hand PH go **SA** 'Dunsden Green 2, Sonning 4¼'.

20 At X-roads after 1½ miles turn **L** 'Binfield Heath, Henley'.

21 Go past Bottle & Glass PH, following signs for Henley, ignoring turns to right and left.

22 At T-j at bottom of hill after passing golf club turn **R** 'Henley 1½'.

23 At T-j with main road by Three Horseshoes PH turn **L** (NS) to return to start in centre of Henley.

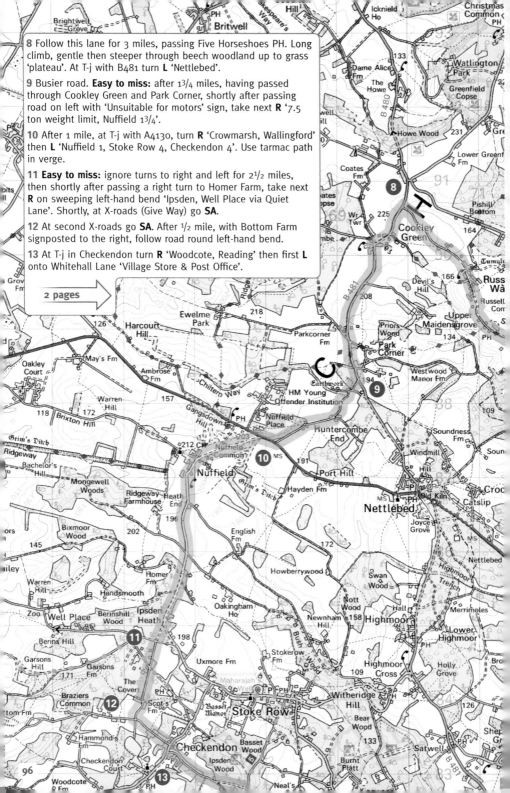

8 Follow this lane for 3 miles, passing Five Horseshoes PH. Long climb, gentle then steeper through beech woodland up to grass 'plateau'. At T-j with B481 turn **L** 'Nettlebed'.

9 Busier road. **Easy to miss:** after 1¾ miles, having passed through Cookley Green and Park Corner, shortly after passing road on left with 'Unsuitable for motors' sign, take next **R** '7.5 ton weight limit, Nuffield 1¾'.

10 After 1 mile, at T-j with A4130, turn **R** 'Crowmarsh, Wallingford' then **L** 'Nuffield 1, Stoke Row 4, Checkendon 4'. Use tarmac path in verge.

11 **Easy to miss:** ignore turns to right and left for 2½ miles, then shortly after passing a right turn to Homer Farm, take next **R** on sweeping left-hand bend 'Ipsden, Well Place via Quiet Lane'. Shortly, at X-roads (Give Way) go **SA**.

12 At second X-roads go **SA**. After ½ mile, with Bottom Farm signposted to the right, follow road round left-hand bend.

13 At T-j in Checkendon turn **R** 'Woodcote, Reading' then first **L** onto Whitehall Lane 'Village Store & Post Office'.

2 pages

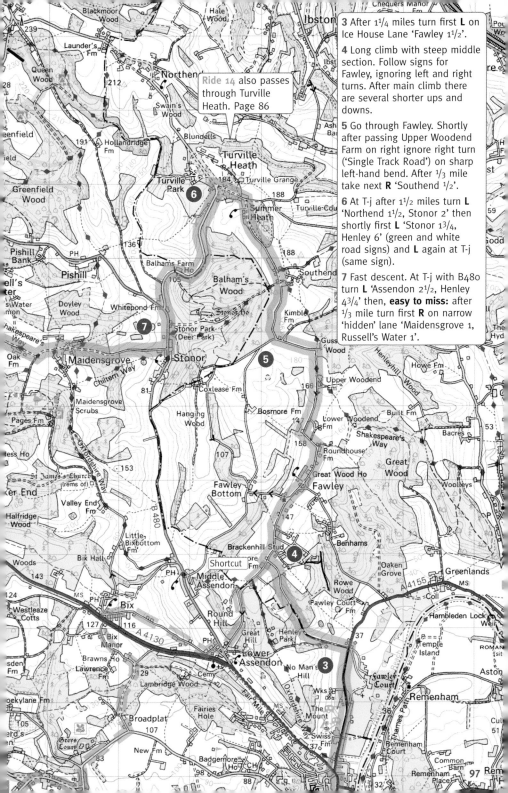

Ride 14 also passes through Turville Heath. Page 86

3 After 1¼ miles turn first **L** on Ice House Lane 'Fawley 1½'.

4 Long climb with steep middle section. Follow signs for Fawley, ignoring left and right turns. After main climb there are several shorter ups and downs.

5 Go through Fawley. Shortly after passing Upper Woodend Farm on right ignore right turn ('Single Track Road') on sharp left-hand bend. After ⅓ mile take next **R** 'Southend ½'.

6 At T-j after 1½ miles turn **L** 'Northend 1½, Stonor 2' then shortly first **L** 'Stonor 1¾, Henley 6' (green and white road signs) and **L** again at T-j (same sign).

7 Fast descent. At T-j with B480 turn **L** 'Assendon 2½, Henley 4¾' then, **easy to miss:** after ⅓ mile turn first **R** on narrow 'hidden' lane 'Maidensgrove 1, Russell's Water 1'.

Lambourn, Wayland's Smithy & Fox Hill

This is one of three rides that use a section of the Ridgeway. Lambourn is one of the country's top training centres for racehorses and you will see a lot of thin men and fast horses on the gallops that encircle the town. One of the problems for mountain bike rides in the area is that all the grassy tracks linking the town to the Ridgeway are no fun as climbs, hence the use of a lane to gain height on

Blowingstone Hill. Climb on broad tracks up past gallops and the Jockey Club Estates

to join the road towards Kingston Lisle. Climb up to the Ridgeway and turn west for some fine easy riding on broad well-maintained tracks passing Uffington Castle and White Horse Hill before a belter of a descent down past Wayland's Smithy, an atmospheric long barrow in a small woodland just off the Ridgeway. The surface of the Ridgeway is smooth stone for much of the way meaning you eat up the miles before turning for home on a rough grassy track parallel with the M4. Tarmac leads to Baydon Hole and a last blast on good stone track back to the start.

Overview

Off-road ● 18 miles / 30 kilometres ● Moderate

Start
Centre of Lambourn, east of Swindon

Parking
Free car park on the B4000 heading south from the centre of the village

Terrain
One long climb (425ft/ 130m) from Lambourn up to the highpoint at Uffington Castle. Several shorter climbs

Nearest railway
Hungerford

Refreshments
Lambourn
Lots of choice

North of the Ridgeway
There are pubs in most of the nearby villages if you descend north from the Ridgeway

Other rides nearby

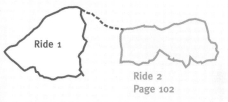

Ride 1

Ride 2
Page 102

Map pages

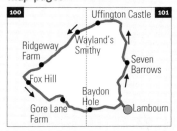

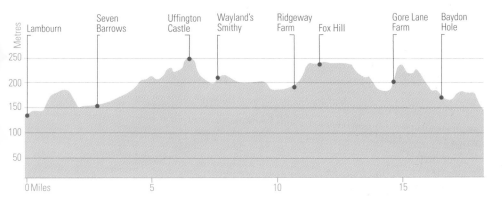

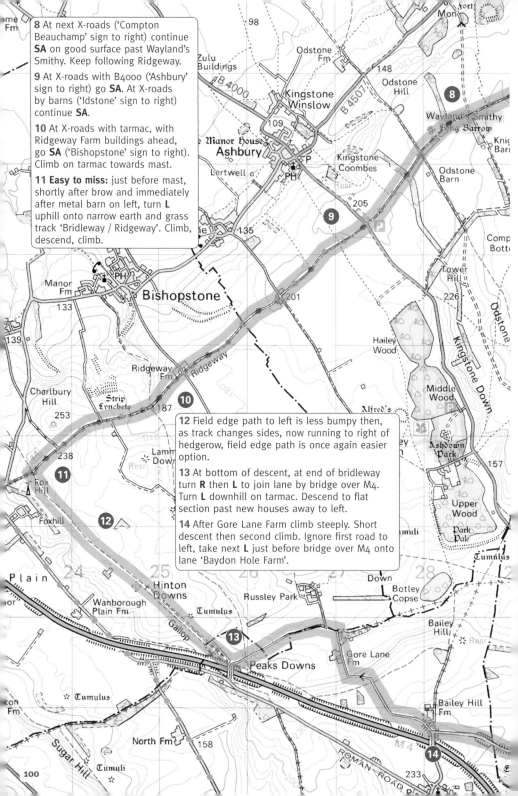

8 At next X-roads ('Compton Beauchamp' sign to right) continue **SA** on good surface past Wayland's Smithy. Keep following Ridgeway.

9 At X-roads with B4000 ('Ashbury' sign to right) go **SA**. At X-roads by barns ('Idstone' sign to right) continue **SA**.

10 At X-roads with tarmac, with Ridgeway Farm buildings ahead, go **SA** ('Bishopstone' sign to right). Climb on tarmac towards mast.

11 Easy to miss: just before mast, shortly after brow and immediately after metal barn on left, turn **L** uphill onto narrow earth and grass track 'Bridleway / Ridgeway'. Climb, descend, climb.

12 Field edge path to left is less bumpy then, as track changes sides, now running to right of hedgerow, field edge path is once again easier option.

13 At bottom of descent, at end of bridleway turn **R** then **L** to join lane by bridge over M4. Turn **L** downhill on tarmac. Descend to flat section past new houses away to left.

14 After Gore Lane Farm climb steeply. Short descent then second climb. Ignore first road to left, take next **L** just before bridge over M4 onto lane 'Baydon Hole Farm'.

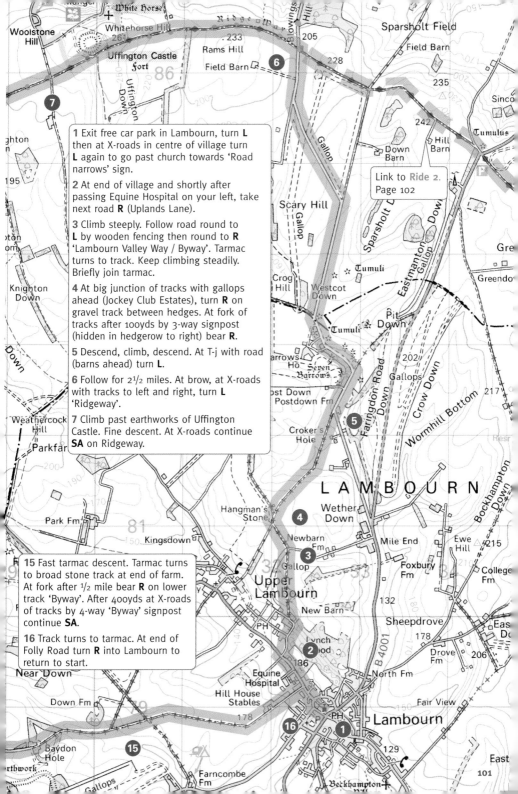

1 Exit free car park in Lambourn, turn **L** then at X-roads in centre of village turn **L** again to go past church towards 'Road narrows' sign.

2 At end of village and shortly after passing Equine Hospital on your left, take next road **R** (Uplands Lane).

3 Climb steeply. Follow road round to **L** by wooden fencing then round to **R** 'Lambourn Valley Way / Byway'. Tarmac turns to track. Keep climbing steadily. Briefly join tarmac.

4 At big junction of tracks with gallops ahead (Jockey Club Estates), turn **R** on gravel track between hedges. At fork of tracks after 100yds by 3-way signpost (hidden in hedgerow to right) bear **R**.

5 Descend, climb, descend. At T-j with road (barns ahead) turn **L**.

6 Follow for 2½ miles. At brow, at X-roads with tracks to left and right, turn **L** 'Ridgeway'.

7 Climb past earthworks of Uffington Castle. Fine descent. At X-roads continue **SA** on Ridgeway.

15 Fast tarmac descent. Tarmac turns to broad stone track at end of farm. At fork after ½ mile bear **R** on lower track 'Byway'. After 400yds at X-roads of tracks by 4-way 'Byway' signpost continue **SA**.

16 Track turns to tarmac. At end of Folly Road turn **R** into Lambourn to return to start.

Link to **Ride 2**. Page 102

West Ilsley & the Ridgeway south of Wantage

The villages of East and West Ilsley are convenient starting points for rides along the Ridgeway as they both lie just off the A34 between Oxford and Newbury. The scenery is one of wide open fields, big skies, training gallops for the horses and clumps of predominantly beech broadleaf woodland, with big views north across the Vale of White Horse. As ever the challenge is trying to turn a linear ride along the Ridgeway into a circular ride, in this case a fine mix of quiet lanes and woodland tracks do the trick. Off-road tracks start as soon as you leave the pub in West Ilsley on a climb up alongside the gallops. The track quality improves as you join the Ridgeway and head west. If the day is fine, the tracks are dry and you are feeling good you can easily turn this into a much longer ride by following the Ridgeway west for many miles. The roughest riding of the day comes soon after leaving the Ridgeway but you have gravity on your side. A mix of carefully chosen lanes and woodland tracks cuts across the grain of the land leading you back to the bright lights of West Ilsley.

Overview
Off-road ● 20 miles / 32 kilometres ● Moderate / Strenuous

Start
Harrow pub, West Ilsley, off the A34 to the southwest of Didcot

Parking
On the road between the pub and the village hall in West Ilsley

Terrain
One long climb, steep at first, from the start to the Ridgeway. Undulating along Ridgeway. Second climb east of the A338 near South Fawley

Nearest railway
Didcot or more fun from Goring via Streatley and the Ridgeway

Refreshments
West Ilsley
Harrow Inn
T: 01635 281260

A338 south of Wantage
(about 1/3 mile north of route)
The Barn Café, Court Hill Centre
T: 01235 760253

Other rides nearby

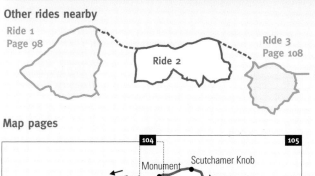

Ride 1
Page 98

Ride 2

Ride 3
Page 108

Map pages

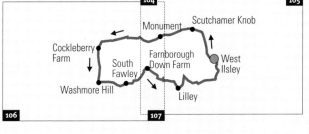

104 · 105 · Scutchamer Knob · Monument · Cockleberry Farm · Farnborough Down Farm · West Ilsley · South Fawley · Washmore Hill · Lilley · 106 · 107

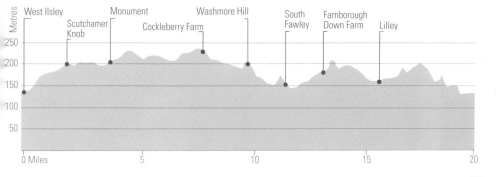

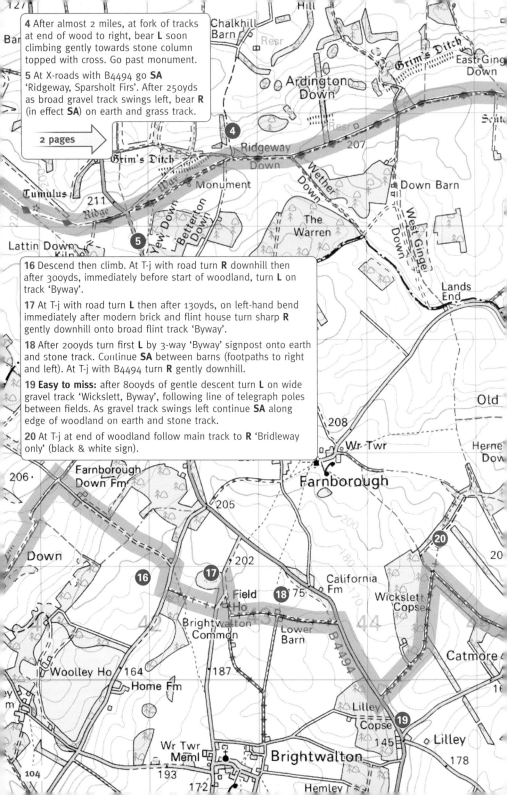

4 After almost 2 miles, at fork of tracks at end of wood to right, bear **L** soon climbing gently towards stone column topped with cross. Go past monument.

5 At X-roads with B4494 go **SA** 'Ridgeway, Sparsholt Firs'. After 250yds as broad gravel track swings left, bear **R** (in effect **SA**) on earth and grass track.

2 pages

16 Descend then climb. At T-j with road turn **R** downhill then after 300yds, immediately before start of woodland, turn **L** on track 'Byway'.

17 At T-j with road turn **L** then after 130yds, on left-hand bend immediately after modern brick and flint house turn sharp **R** gently downhill onto broad flint track 'Byway'.

18 After 200yds turn first **L** by 3-way 'Byway' signpost onto earth and stone track. Continue **SA** between barns (footpaths to right and left). At T-j with B4494 turn **R** gently downhill.

19 Easy to miss: after 800yds of gentle descent turn **L** on wide gravel track 'Wickslett, Byway', following line of telegraph poles between fields. As gravel track swings left continue **SA** along edge of woodland on earth and stone track.

20 At T-j at end of woodland follow main track to **R** 'Bridleway only' (black & white sign).

Link to **Ride 3**.
Page 108

1 With your back to Harrow pub in West Ilsley turn **R** 'Farnborough, Wantage' then immediately turn **R** again onto broad gravel track opposite cricket ground 'Bridleway only'. After 600yds at fork of two wide chalk tracks bear **L** (blue arrow) on less steep option. Short tough climb on chalk.

2 Chalk turns to grass (gallops to right). Climb gently for just over 1 mile, at times bumpy. Cross gallops by white posts. At T-j with Ridgeway turn **L** on broad chalk and flint track.

3 At X-roads shortly after small car parking area to left, and small wood ahead, go **SA** 'Ridgeway'. Continue in same direction on long, flat section on earth and grass then chalk and flint, ignoring turns to right and left.

21 At X-roads with lane turn **R** then immediately **L** onto wide stone track 'Byway'. Ignore first bridleway to left on right-hand bend. After 150yds turn **L** into woodland on broad gravel track 'Byway'. Briefly exit woodland, following track and blue arrows to **R** at end of small field to re-enter woodland.

22 Long descent (may be muddy at bottom) then short climb. At T-j turn **L** 'Byway' then **easy to miss** after 150yds turn **L** again downhill on similar track 'Bridleway'. Shortly at 3-way 'Footpath / Bridleway' sign turn **R** on rough grass track.

23 Keep following blue arrows and 'Bridleway' signs as rough grass turns to chalk then gravel. At T-j with tarmac turn **L**. At next T-j with flint wall ahead turn **L** for 600yds to return to start.

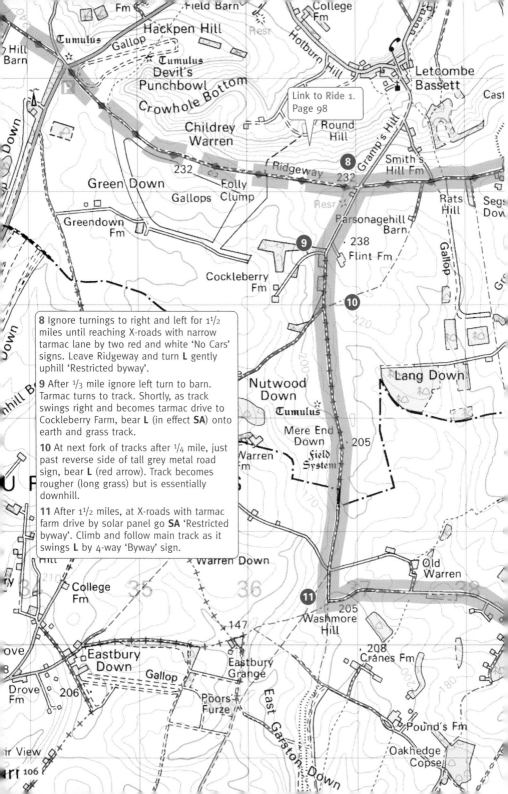

Link to **Ride 1**.
Page 98

8 Ignore turnings to right and left for 1½ miles until reaching X-roads with narrow tarmac lane by two red and white 'No Cars' signs. Leave Ridgeway and turn **L** gently uphill 'Restricted byway'.

9 After ⅓ mile ignore left turn to barn. Tarmac turns to track. Shortly, as track swings right and becomes tarmac drive to Cockleberry Farm, bear **L** (in effect **SA**) onto earth and grass track.

10 At next fork of tracks after ¼ mile, just past reverse side of tall grey metal road sign, bear **L** (red arrow). Track becomes rougher (long grass) but is essentially downhill.

11 After 1½ miles, at X-roads with tarmac farm drive by solar panel go **SA** 'Restricted byway'. Climb and follow main track as it swings **L** by 4-way 'Byway' sign.

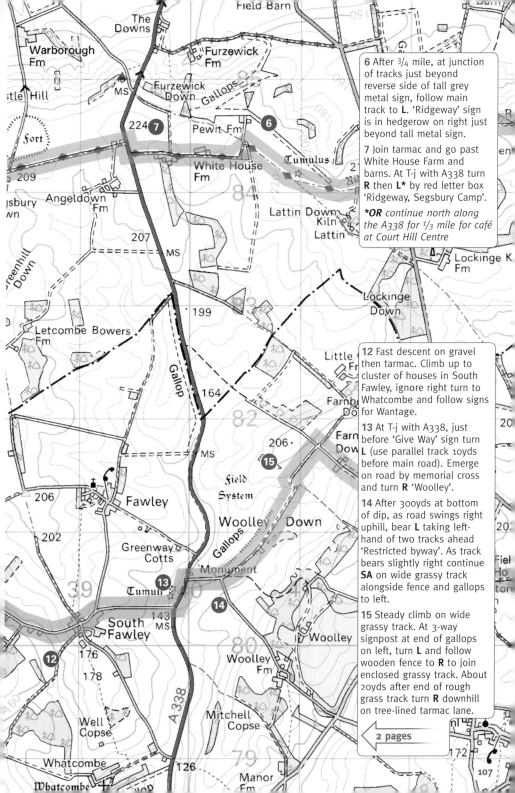

6 After 3/4 mile, at junction of tracks just beyond reverse side of tall grey metal sign, follow main track to **L**. 'Ridgeway' sign is in hedgerow on right just beyond tall metal sign.

7 Join tarmac and go past White House Farm and barns. At T-j with A338 turn **R** then **L*** by red letter box 'Ridgeway, Segsbury Camp'.

*OR continue north along the A338 for 1/3 mile for café at Court Hill Centre

12 Fast descent on gravel then tarmac. Climb up to cluster of houses in South Fawley, ignore right turn to Whatcombe and follow signs for Wantage.

13 At T-j with A338, just before 'Give Way' sign turn **L** (use parallel track 10yds before main road). Emerge on road by memorial cross and turn **R** 'Woolley'.

14 After 300yds at bottom of dip, as road swings right uphill, bear **L** taking left-hand of two tracks ahead 'Restricted byway'. As track bears slightly right continue **SA** on wide grassy track alongside fence and gallops to left.

15 Steady climb on wide grassy track. At 3-way signpost at end of gallops on left, turn **L** and follow wooden fence to **R** to join enclosed grassy track. About 20yds after end of rough grass track turn **R** downhill on tree-lined tarmac lane.

← **2 pages**

107

East of Streatley on the Ridgeway to East Ilsley

This "balloon with a string" shaped ride climbs up from the Thames Valley at Streatley where the river cuts its way through the chalk at the famous Goring Gap (before it did this the Thames used to join the sea at the Wash). To the east of the Thames are the thickly wooded slopes of the Chilterns, whereas to the west of the river lie the big open spaces and wide chalk and flint tracks of the Ridgeway and the Berkshire / Wiltshire Downs. Climb steadily on the broad chalk and flint track from Warren Farm, gaining 300ft (90m), keeping in mind the fact that you have this to look forward to as a descent at the end of the ride. East Ilsley offers refreshments at a couple

of pubs. Soon after leaving East Ilsley you leave the broad chalk tracks that have characterised the ride so far for some good singletrack which may become overgrown at the height of summer. Descend to cross the infant River Pang, then climb 330ft

(100m) from the lowest to the highest point of the ride, above Aldworth, setting you up for a long easy descent back to the start along the outward route.

NB The area is packed full of byways and bridleways. If the conditions are fast and dry and you are feeling strong, it would be very easy to link to Ride 2 in West Ilsley and indeed to Ride 1 as well. The tracks change dramatically from summer to winter and the same ride may take three times as long in wet and muddy winter conditions as it would do after a hot dry spell in summer.

Overview
Off-road ● 17 miles / 28 kilometres ● Moderate

Start
Warren Farm, off the A417 to
the northwest of Streatley

Parking
Turn off the A417 Streatley
- Wantage road about 1/2
mile north of Streatley onto
Rectory Road signposted
'Golf course'. After 1 1/2 miles
turn right opposite a large
thatched house onto a broad
track signposted 'Ridgeway'.
Park here

Terrain
Two main climbs: the first
(300ft / 90m) from the start
up onto the Ridgeway and
the second (330ft / 100m) to
the northwest of Hampstead
Norreys. Several other shorter
climbs

Nearest railway
Goring

Other rides nearby

Ride 2
Page 102

Refreshments

East Ilsley
Crown & Horns PH
T: 01635 281545
Swan PH
T: 01635 281238

Aldworth
Bell PH
T: 01635 578272

Map pages

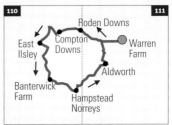

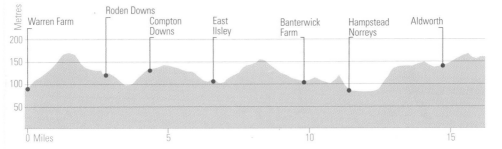

109

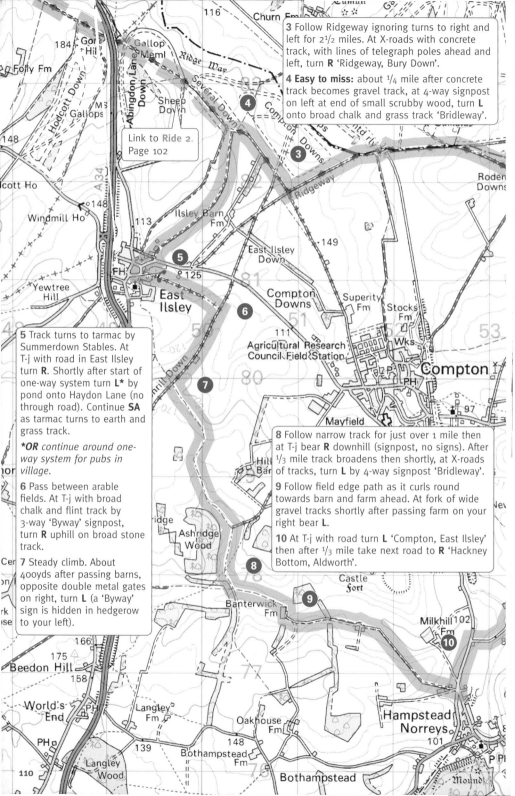

3 Follow Ridgeway ignoring turns to right and left for 2½ miles. At X-roads with concrete track, with lines of telegraph poles ahead and left, turn **R** 'Ridgeway, Bury Down'.

4 Easy to miss: about ¼ mile after concrete track becomes gravel track, at 4-way signpost on left at end of small scrubby wood, turn **L** onto broad chalk and grass track 'Bridleway'.

Link to **Ride 2**.
Page 102

5 Track turns to tarmac by Summerdown Stables. At T-j with road in East Ilsley turn **R**. Shortly after start of one-way system turn **L*** by pond onto Haydon Lane (no through road). Continue **SA** as tarmac turns to earth and grass track.

***OR** continue around one-way system for pubs in village.*

6 Pass between arable fields. At T-j with broad chalk and flint track by 3-way 'Byway' signpost, turn **R** uphill on broad stone track.

7 Steady climb. About 400yds after passing barns, opposite double metal gates on right, turn **L** (a 'Byway' sign is hidden in hedgerow to your left).

8 Follow narrow track for just over 1 mile then at T-j bear **R** downhill (signpost, no signs). After ⅓ mile track broadens then shortly, at X-roads of tracks, turn **L** by 4-way signpost 'Bridleway'.

9 Follow field edge path as it curls round towards barn and farm ahead. At fork of wide gravel tracks shortly after passing farm on your right bear **L**.

10 At T-j with road turn **L** 'Compton, East Ilsley' then after ⅓ mile take next road to **R** 'Hackney Bottom, Aldworth'.

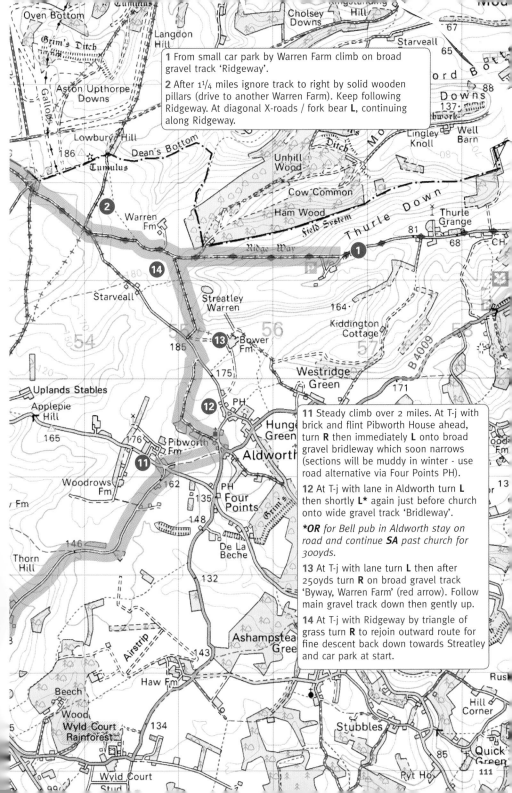

1 From small car park by Warren Farm climb on broad gravel track 'Ridgeway'.

2 After 1¼ miles ignore track to right by solid wooden pillars (drive to another Warren Farm). Keep following Ridgeway. At diagonal X-roads / fork bear **L**, continuing along Ridgeway.

11 Steady climb over 2 miles. At T-j with brick and flint Pibworth House ahead, turn **R** then immediately **L** onto broad gravel bridleway which soon narrows (sections will be muddy in winter - use road alternative via Four Points PH).

12 At T-j with lane in Aldworth turn **L** then shortly **L*** again just before church onto wide gravel track 'Bridleway'.

***OR** for Bell pub in Aldworth stay on road and continue **SA** past church for 300yds.*

13 At T-j with lane turn **L** then after 250yds turn **R** on broad gravel track 'Byway, Warren Farm' (red arrow). Follow main gravel track down then gently up.

14 At T-j with Ridgeway by triangle of grass turn **R** to rejoin outward route for fine descent back down towards Streatley and car park at start.

Watlington, Maidensgrove & the Chiltern Woodlands

The Ridgeway is claimed to be the oldest road in Europe, dating back some 5000 years. At this point it is also known as the Icknield Way, named after the Iceni tribe which inhabited Norfolk before the arrival of the Romans. The track climbs steeply through Howe Wood up to Cookley Green, the highest point on the ride. After Russell's Water you enter the secret kingdom of the Chilterns with a lofty canopy of beech trees covering the steep hillsides and dry valleys linked by a magnificent network of bridleways. After the steady climb to Park Corner the trail becomes slightly less defined on its gentle descent through woodland back into the open farmland which characterises the start of the ride.

NB As with all rides in the Chilterns, this can be very tough going from late autumn to late spring when many of the tracks turn to mud.

Overview
Off-road ● 15 miles / 24 kilometres ● Strenuous

Start
The free car park in Watlington - follow signs

Parking
As above

Terrain
Three main climbs - from Ewelme to Cookley Green (430ft /130m); from Pishill to Maidensgrove (230ft / 70m) and from Maidensgrove to Park Corner (300ft / 90m)

Nearest railway
Henley

Refreshments
Watlington
Lots of choice

Other rides nearby

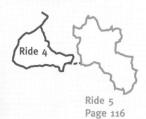

Ride 4

Ride 5
Page 116

Map pages

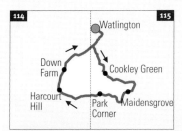

114 115
Watlington
Down Farm
Cookley Green
Harcourt Hill
Park Corner
Maidensgrove

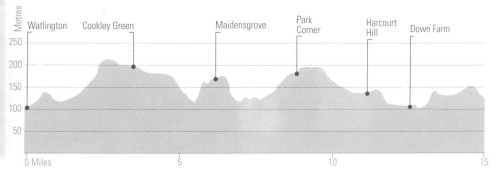

12 Long, gentle descent over 1¹/₄ miles. At T-j with broad gravel track turn **L** then at T-j with tarmac turn **R** 'Byway' (purple arrow) following telegraph poles.

13 Tarmac soon turns to track after houses. Climb on wide track with open field to left and hedge to right. **Easy to miss:** after ¹/₂ mile, towards top of climb and about 200yds before woodland starts ahead, turn **R** uphill through wide gap in hedgerow (wooden post with blue arrows is tucked in behind hedge).

14 Climb then descend. At X-roads of tracks at bottom of dip, go **SA** uphill (blue arrow). After ¹/₂ mile at X-roads with tarmac go **SA**.

15 Follow field edge. At T-j with road turn **R**, then on right-hand bend bear **L** 'Restricted Byway'. Continue **SA** past tall red & white 'No cars' sign.

16 At T-j with broad gravel track bear **R** (in effect **SA**). At X-roads with lane go **SA** 'Ridgeway, Watlington 1'.

17 Keep following 'Ridgeway' signs. Rejoin outward route. At X-roads with B480 go **SA** onto track by letterbox. At T-j with road turn **L** downhill to return to car park at start in Watlington.

1 Exit car park in Watlington, turn **R** uphill. After ¹/₂ mile, just before gradient steepens turn **R** on Ridgeway.

2 At X-roads with B480 go **SA** 'Dame Alice Farm'. After ¹/₄ mile at 5-way junction turn **L** on tarmac lane 'Bridleway'. After ¹/₄ mile as road swings right into farm bear **L** onto woodland track.

3 Long steady woodland climb, following white arrows painted on trees. At T-j with tarmac (with Woods Farm to right) turn **L** then at X-roads with road turn **L** again ('Private Road to Coates Farm' ahead).

4 Shortly at T-j with busier road (B480) turn **R**. Ignore first left to Stonor. After ¹/₄ mile take next **L** 'Russell's Water ³/₄, Maidensgrove 2'.

5 Gentle descent over ³/₄ mile. Just after row of semi-detached red-brick houses and before pond turn **L** by tall 'Russell's Water' village sign. Go **SA** at 'Farm Access Only' sign to pass between barns. Go **SA** onto narrow grassy track which soon improves, following white arrows.

6 Fine descent on smooth woodland track. At T-j of tracks near to house turn sharp **R** 'PS17' (blue arrow).

7 Fine views. Steep descent then steep climb. Continue on track through woodland following white arrows and ignoring turnings to left then right. At T-j with road turn **R** uphill.

8 Ignore left turn ('Maidensgrove only'). Exit woodland. On sharp right-hand bend at far side of wide, flat, grassy area leave road and bear **L** (in effect **SA**) onto track 'Restricted Byway, Chiltern Way'.

9 Fast descent. At X-roads of tracks at bottom turn **R**.

10 Long woodland climb. Ignore right turn on exit from woodland. Follow concrete road to pass to **R** of farm.

11 After almost 1 mile, at T-j with tarmac with house called Westray ahead bear **L**. At T-j with B481 turn **R** then **L** onto track 'Bridleway to Ewelme'. At X-roads with wide farm track go **SA** onto similar woodland track.

Link to Ride 5. Page 116

From Hambleden into the heart of the Chilterns

As with so much of the off-road cycling in the Chilterns, it is astonishing how far you feel from the built-up South East on this ride. Only 30 miles from central London, you could easily convince yourself you are deep in the West Country. The ride starts from near the Thames at Mill End and climbs on road for 3½ miles through Rotten Row and Rockwell End to Parmoor. A superb descent follows, dropping down through Hatchet Wood to Skirmett and Fingest, with both villages boasting fine pubs. Three steep climbs and descents in and out of the beechwoods take you to Northend and the highest point on the ride. Appropriately this is followed by the longest descent, down to Stonor and then the steepest climb alongside the park boundary. From the top the views across the Thames valley to the southeast are magnificent and with the exception of a very short climb near to the end the ride is all downhill.

Overview
Off-road ● 18 miles / 30 kilometres ● Strenuous

Start
The car park 3 miles northeast of Henley just off the A4155 Marlow road on the minor road towards Hambleden and Skirmett

Parking
As above

Terrain
Hilly with five climbs of 300-430ft (90-130m)

Nearest railway
Henley

Other rides nearby

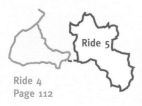

Ride 5

Ride 4
Page 112

Refreshments

Hambleden
Stag & Huntsman PH
T: 01491 571227

Skirmett
Frog PH
T: 01491 638996

Fingest
Chequers Inn
T: 01491 638335

Turville
Bull & Butcher PH
T: 01491 638283

Map pages

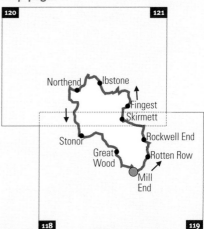

120   121

Northend   Ibstone
Fingest
Skirmett
Stonor   Rockwell End
Great Wood   Rotten Row
Mill End

118   119

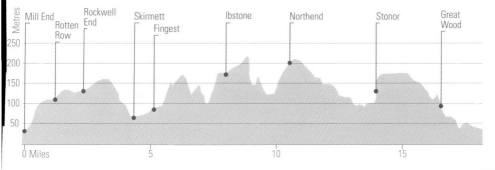

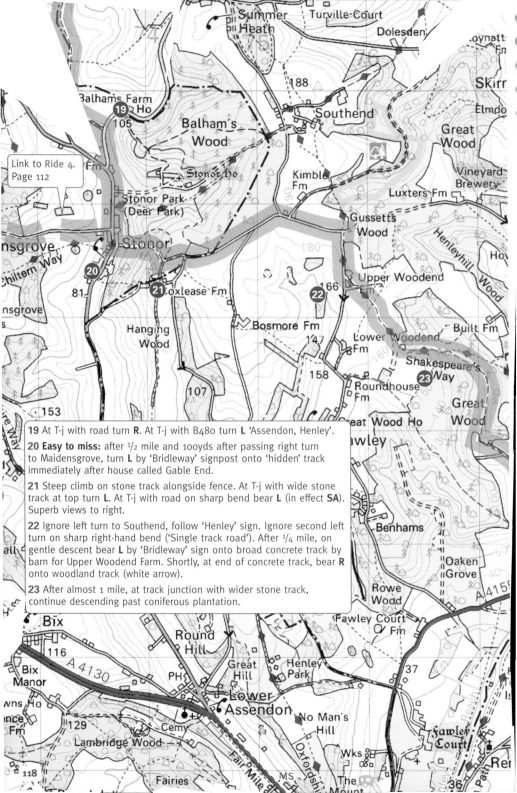

Link to **Ride** 4.
Page 112

19 At T-j with road turn **R**. At T-j with B480 turn **L** 'Assendon, Henley'.

20 Easy to miss: after ¹/₂ mile and 100yds after passing right turn to Maidensgrove, turn **L** by 'Bridleway' signpost onto 'hidden' track immediately after house called Gable End.

21 Steep climb on stone track alongside fence. At T-j with wide stone track at top turn **L**. At T-j with road on sharp bend bear **L** (in effect **SA**). Superb views to right.

22 Ignore left turn to Southend, follow 'Henley' sign. Ignore second left turn on sharp right-hand bend ('Single track road'). After ¹/₄ mile, on gentle descent bear **L** by 'Bridleway' sign onto broad concrete track by barn for Upper Woodend Farm. Shortly, at end of concrete track, bear **R** onto woodland track (white arrow).

23 After almost 1 mile, at track junction with wider stone track, continue descending past coniferous plantation.

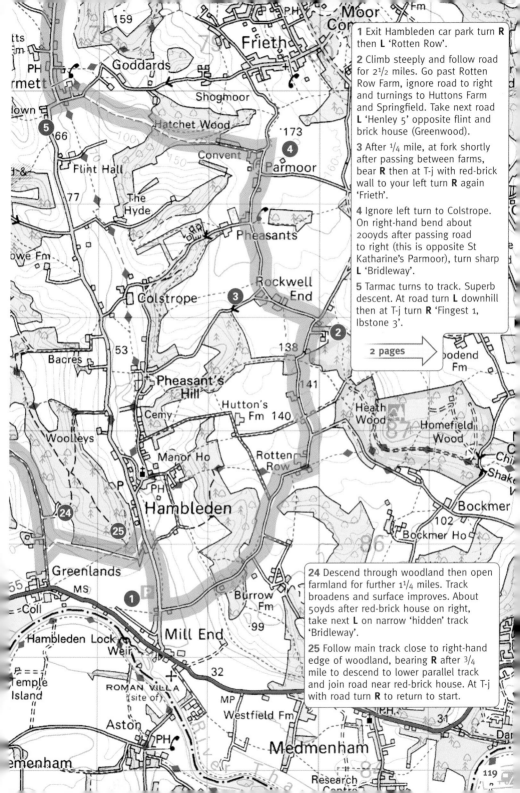

1 Exit Hambleden car park turn **R** then **L** 'Rotten Row'.

2 Climb steeply and follow road for 2½ miles. Go past Rotten Row Farm, ignore road to right and turnings to Huttons Farm and Springfield. Take next road **L** 'Henley 5' opposite flint and brick house (Greenwood).

3 After ¼ mile, at fork shortly after passing between farms, bear **R** then at T-j with red-brick wall to your left turn **R** again 'Frieth'.

4 Ignore left turn to Colstrope. On right-hand bend about 200yds after passing road to right (this is opposite St Katharine's Parmoor), turn sharp **L** 'Bridleway'.

5 Tarmac turns to track. Superb descent. At road turn **L** downhill then at T-j turn **R** 'Fingest 1, Ibstone 3'.

> 2 pages →

24 Descend through woodland then open farmland for further 1¼ miles. Track broadens and surface improves. About 50yds after red-brick house on right, take next **L** on narrow 'hidden' track 'Bridleway'.

25 Follow main track close to right-hand edge of woodland, bearing **R** after ¾ mile to descend to lower parallel track and join road near red-brick house. At T-j with road turn **R** to return to start.

12 Ignore left turn ('Unsuitable for HGVs'). After 3/4 mile at X-roads (your priority) turn **L** onto Grays Lane (no through road). Shortly, just before cricket pitch, fork **R** onto smooth grass track.

13 After 1/4 mile as main track swings left, turn **R** along rough field edge 'Bridleway'. **Easy to miss:** after 200yds turn **L** on narrow track into woodland and immediately bear **L** downhill towards arrow on tree.

14 Fine singletrack descent. Shortly after exit from wood, at end of wire fence, turn sharp **L** following fence around corner.

15 At T-j with road turn **L** then immediately **R** onto grassy track. Steep climb through woodland. At T-j with tarmac turn **L** to continue climbing.

16 At road junction turn **R** and **R** again uphill 'Christmas Common 1 1/4'. **Easy to miss:** after 1/2 mile, just after house called Badgerbury on left and just before '7.5 ton weight limit' sign, turn **L** into woodland 'Permissive bridleway'.

17 Go through metal bridlegate and with red-brick building ahead turn sharp **L** between hedges. After 3/4 mile at X-roads at bottom turn **L** to continue downhill.

18 Long descent following white arrows, ignoring turnings to right and left. Surface turns from stone to grass after farm buildings then improves to fine, broad, gravel track.

19 At T-j with road turn **R**. At T-j with B480 turn **L** 'Assendon, Henley'.

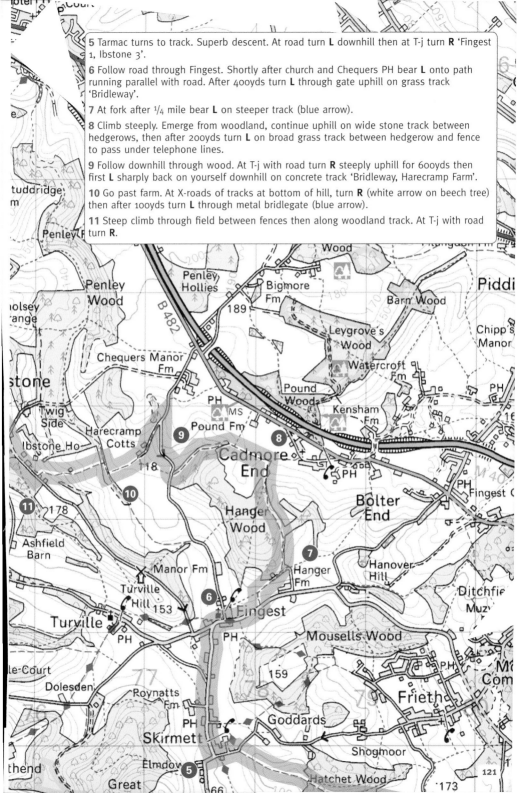

5 Tarmac turns to track. Superb descent. At road turn **L** downhill then at T-j turn **R** 'Fingest 1, Ibstone 3'.

6 Follow road through Fingest. Shortly after church and Chequers PH bear **L** onto path running parallel with road. After 400yds turn **L** through gate uphill on grass track 'Bridleway'.

7 At fork after ¼ mile bear **L** on steeper track (blue arrow).

8 Climb steeply. Emerge from woodland, continue uphill on wide stone track between hedgerows, then after 200yds turn **L** on broad grass track between hedgerow and fence to pass under telephone lines.

9 Follow downhill through wood. At T-j with road turn **R** steeply uphill for 600yds then first **L** sharply back on yourself downhill on concrete track 'Bridleway, Harecramp Farm'.

10 Go past farm. At X-roads of tracks at bottom of hill, turn **R** (white arrow on beech tree) then after 100yds turn **L** through metal bridlegate (blue arrow).

11 Steep climb through field between fences then along woodland track. At T-j with road turn **R**.